Motorcycle Camping
Made Easy

SECOND EDITION

Bob Woofter

Whitehorse Press
Center Conway, New Hampshire

Whitehorse Press books are also available at discounts in bulk quantity for sales and promotional use. For details about special sales or for a catalog of Whitehorse Press motorcycling books, write to the publisher:

Whitehorse Press
107 East Conway Road
Center Conway, New Hampshire 03813
Phone: 603-356-6556 or 800-531-1133
E-mail: CustomerService@WhitehorsePress.com
Internet: www.WhitehorsePress.com

ISBN: 1-884313-83-3
ISBN-13: 978-1-884313-83-7

5   4

Printed in the United States of America

Sitting with good friends around a camp fire— it doesn't get any better than this. Photo by Ron Smith

Dancing on the Dragon's Tail. Photo courtesy of Deals Gap Motorcycle Resort

Camping is wonderful—as are grandchildren. This book is dedicated to all my current grandchildren, Erica, Clayton, Austin, Nathan, and Logan, and all my future grandchildren in the hopes that they, too, will someday learn the joys of campcraft and motorcycles.

As a nod to the intrepid campers and outdoorsmen who
came a century (and in one case 500 years) before us,
throughout this book in the margins you'll find
one hundred and one snippets of outdoor wisdom
that were once deemed common knowledge.
Some are nutty and entertaining, while others
are as true today as they were then.
I hope you'll enjoy them as much
as I have. Can you spot the one
that is five centuries old?

*Photo by Jim Woofter, 1915 Austro Omega motorcycle
courtesy Bruce Williams, Cortland, Ohio.*

Table of Contents

Preface

At the time I wrote the first edition of *Motorcycle Camping Made Easy*, no book had been published on the subject of motorcycle camping for 28 years. From my own experience as a life-long camper I believed then that a new book was long overdue and that there was a waiting audience of bike campers and wanna-be campers eager for a comprehensive guide to camping in general and motorcycle camping in particular. I wasn't wrong. I'm happy to say that *Motorcycle Camping Made Easy* has been one of this publisher's successful books. Its sales remained consistently strong and its appeal broad . . . world-wide, in fact.

No one knows for sure how many motorcycle campers there are in the world, much less how many would like to be motorcycle campers, but it is for those folks this book was written. It's for the folks who enjoy touring on blacktop, have cell phones, and appreciate not having to kill and skin their supper. These folks enjoy camp cooking but also appreciate the convenience of an occasional fast burger and slice of pie at the local diner. In short, this book is written for folks who want to feel comfortable while camping, and not challenged. Motorcycle camping, as I intend you to know it, is a civilized and enjoyable experience—one that on cold winter nights will stir fond reminiscences of past trips and eager anticipation of future ventures.

Cargo, er, bambino trailer, Italian style, circa 1950.

Acknowledgments

Though readers will often skim over the Acknowledgments, this author knows that creating a work that is polished, professional, entertaining, and useful to readers is a team effort. For me the team has been a couple of editors at Whitehorse Press, Lisa Dionne (first edition editor), Sarah Kimball (current editor), Molly Dore (book designer), along with publishers Dan and Judy Kennedy and the entire staff at Whitehorse Press. Thank you all.

I'm also indebted to my many fellow motorcycle camping friends as well as motorcycle campground owners who have once again contributed many fine images. It just wouldn't be the same without you.

Motorcycle camping can give you the freedom to explore wild remote places.

Introduction

Since this book was first published in 2002, much has changed in the realm of motorcycle camping, or has it? Certainly our basic interest hasn't; after a century of motorcycling we're still participating in what has remained one of its most enjoyable adjuncts—camping. Also remaining unchanged are the basic techniques of camping.

What has changed is much of the gear involved, and especially the marketing of it. Manufacturers, and those purporting to be manufacturers of gear, have slicked up their marketing programs with a mind-boggling cornucopia of new terminology that leaves prospective buyers utterly bewildered. If this book achieves nothing else it will assist you in making better gear choices, to help your camping experiences be happy ones.

In the years following the first edition of this book I observed that those who enjoyed and appreciated the book most were new to camping. This was very gratifying since my stated goal at that time had been to write the very best all-round motorcycle camping guide that could be found. This remains my goal since I suspect that most motorcyclists have never camped before. I also knew that most bikers are intrigued by camping yet many have shied away from it only because of a lack of camping know-how.

What's a camp without a camp dog?
Photo courtesy of Willville Motorcycle Campground

Brian and Sheryl Batiste are experts at packing motorcycles.

The starting point of this edition then is the same as the last—I assume the reader knows nothing about camping or its adaptation to motorcycles. As the book proceeds I lead the reader, step-by-step, through the process of choosing and acquiring gear, packing and hauling it on a bike, and finally using it in the field. The learning curve is steep, but I hope this book will help to keep it short.

While the basic essentials of recreational camping have remained unchanged since its inception a little more than one hundred years ago, all the technological advancements of the surrounding world seem to be encroaching. However in camping as with all other aspects of life, we need to allow these devices to enhance our experience without detracting from its quality.

Some things the surrounding world and all its technologies cannot change. Among these is the immense gratification that comes from sitting with friends around an evening campfire. It may sound trite in this day and age, but it's unfailingly true that it just doesn't get any better than this.

Bob Woofter
May, 2009
Cortland, Ohio

*Linda Knepp of Champion, Ohio, greets a lovely
Canadian morning. Photo by Jim Knepp*

*Wake up to a shoreline breakfast in the
Canadian Rockies. Photo by Lorne Sokoloff*

Why Motorcycle Camp?

As soon as people figured out that messing about with motorcycles was a hoot, camping and motorcycling became inextricably linked. Of course, in the early days, this union was typically of urgent necessity, rather than for the sake of its own enjoyment. The fact is, early motorcycles were so unreliable a rider simply couldn't count on arriving at his destination, least of all returning before dark. Tires, especially, were so crude they might last only a mile or two on the deeply-rutted dirt paths that served as roads. It's almost impossible to imagine, in our current age of cell phones and towing services, that a blowout would require a rider—on the spot—to remove and repair his own tire. Not surprisingly, nightfall found many bikers stranded in the country, and a blanket or waterproof tarp made sleeping alongside the road decidedly more tolerable. Motorcycle "camping" was thus born. Finally, sometime after roads and machines achieved greater dependability, motorcycle camping graduated from a necessary evil to part of the enjoyment of biking.

Still there are many more motorcyclists who don't camp than do. There are those who never ride farther than a couple hours away from their beds. And then there are those who hold that camping is foolhardy when there are perfectly good hotels with nice comfortable beds available for the taking.

I will admit that I have spent a night or two in some pretty swank inns but I still say that by comparison, there is no comparison. For me, camping has them beat, hands down. Okay, I'll grant you that it is impractical to set up a tent on the strip in Vegas or in a big city, but for touring the open road there is no better way of experiencing the countryside and the people, no better way of relaxing and having a blast, than motorcycle camping. To support this claim, let me offer a few reasons why camping can be so appealing.

Camaraderie means enjoying the company of good friends. Photo by Ron Smith

CAMARADERIE

If it's true that all motorcyclists share a bond—witness the custom of passing bikers to wave or nod to each other as a gesture of kinship—then it's even more so with motorcycle campers. It's like belonging to the special forces branch of the military, the guys and gals with special training, special gear, and special assignments. Motorcycle campers are a fraternity—never of strangers, just friends who haven't met yet.

Rally camping is hugely popular with many bikers as it provides the opportunity to socialize with old friends and make new ones. There is absolutely no substitute for sharing good times, good food, tales of the road, and just plain gossip around a campfire. The first motorcycle rally I went to was several hundred miles from home and I knew no one there. Within minutes of arriving, I'd made some good friends that I look forward to seeing at other rallies around the country, even to this day.

The yearly motorcycle gatherings at Sturgis, South Dakota, and Daytona Beach, Florida, attract hundreds of thousands of bikers from all over the world, most of whom are enthusiasts with decades of rally experience. Replete with unending miles of beachside hotels, Bike Week Daytona still hosts many tens of thousands of campers at both its commercial and make-shift campgrounds, while at Sturgis, due to its dearth of hotels, hundreds of acres of pastureland are transformed into veritable seas of camp tents.

Much less well known but oh so popular are Americade, AMA Vintage Days, and the marque rallies such as the Honda Wing Ding, and the BMW International Bike Rallies, which have to be experienced to be appreciated.

~

Always wear a money belt and for money take gold coins rather than paper in case you get a ducking in water.

~

At peace in God's country. Photo by Cindy Sokoloff

I JUST WANT TO BE LEFT ALONE!

The clamor of city life, nerve-wracking commutes, the shrill of televisions and cell phones, the glare of computer screens and the pressures of life in general can cause everyone from time to time to seek the relief that only solitude can bring. Does solo camping in a beautiful forest beside a clear stream appear enticing? It's a reality that many motorcycle campers are able to experience.

FREEDOM

Bikers often talk about the freedom of the road and the freedom of feeling the wind on their faces. For others, this "freedom" is best epitomized by the ability to set off from home with just a sleeping bag and a tent strapped to the back of the bike. Their freedom comes from knowing that even when there may be a definite destination and travel plan, there doesn't have to be. The motorcycle camper can be virtually self-sufficient and free from constraining routes and schedules.

Freedom to a motorcyclist means going wherever the wind and the road take you. Photo by John Cheetham

EXPERIENCE NATURE

For many campers, just being outdoors is reason enough to camp. We have felt the peace and contentment of listening to night sounds while lying in our tents: the gentle chirp of night frogs and toads, the hooting of owls and the rustling of leaves in the breeze. We have also watched countless deer grazing peacefully in a meadow, observed bald eagles swooping down to capture a lake trout, beheld innumerable sunsets and sunrises, and relished the aroma of fresh-brewed coffee on the crisp morning air. Try that from the inside of a Holiday Inn room.

ECONOMICS

In the present climate of economic uncertainty, being cost conscious is no longer a joking matter. With the price of lodging, eating out, and fuel at or near record highs, more travelers than ever are opting for motorcycle camping as a plausible means of maintaining their touring habit.

How cheap is it? The price of a tent campsite in commercial campgrounds such as a KOA will vary from location to location with those in close proximity to major attractions costing more, but in 2008 campers paid roughly $20 to $30 per night.

YOUR VERY OWN ADVENTURE

People love adventure . . . or at least the illusion of it. The success of contemporary "reality-based" movies, television shows, and computer games are just the latest in the evolution of a genre that began, literally, with Stone Age storytelling. However, for those of us not content to experience our adventures through the eyes of others, motorcycle camping provides a way to experience the real thing. What's adventure? For some, it's a weekend in a nearby state park. For others, it's nothing less than a months-long marathon trek from Prudhoe Bay, Alaska, to Tierra del Fuego, Argentina. It's your call.

NECESSITY

Speaking of Tierra del Fuego, your chosen routes may take you into areas where Motel 8s and Holiday Inns are few and far between. In that event it's good to have camping skills and equipment. Another sound reason to camp is if there are simply no lodging vacancies

~

A camp first-aid kit should contain forceps, surgeon's needles, silk thread and two bottles of brandy.

~

14

within a reasonable distance of your destination. It's great to have the camping option in your pocket. Of course this doesn't just occur in undeveloped areas—just ask the thousands of bikers who are forced to camp each year at Daytona and Sturgis!

MEMORIES

When you are back in the "real world" and your camping gear is waiting in the garage for the next trip, you will always have the memories, photos, and stories from the last trip to tide you over.

So you see there are many reasons why people camp. While motivations may be diverse, most campers have two things in common: first, they all derive pleasure from camping and second, none were born knowing how to do it. Make no mistake, proficient camping, like playing the piano, programming a computer, or tailoring a suit, is a skill that requires time to learn. It also requires mentors to teach it, and quality equipment to learn with. Your camping can be made easy too, if you give it time and use this book as your mentor and guide to good equipment. Before long you'll be making your own list of reasons to camp.

~

Second-hand army tents, being well-designed and made, are ideal for camping.

~

Create your own motorcycle adventure. Photo by Ken Gibson

Great destinations for a motorcycle trip exist all over the country. Photo by Jim Woofter

This light bike with camping gear made it to the top of Pike's Peak. Photo by Harlan Crouse

Camping Destinations

A Few Options
to Whet Your Appetite

Tape a map of the world on the wall and throw a dart; it's actually that easy to find a wonderful motorcycle camping destination. But don't be surprised if the place hasn't already had an earlier motorcycle visitor. Since the early 1900s adventuresome folks have been trekking to almost every nook and cranny on the globe. Because an amazing number of these early pioneers as well as modern day riders have documented their exploits both in writing and film, it is quite possible to research places both far away and close to home from the comfort of your armchair.

A good way to discover and explore destination options is to read tour guides, official department of tourism literature, magazine articles, and travelogues. Because they're written from a personal perspective, travelogues allow you to learn aspects of a region's culture and geography as seen through the eyes of the writer.

Travelogues that were written in what are now considered the vintage days of motorcycling are wonderfully entertaining as well as instructive. It's truly amazing to see the places where these men and women ventured with their machines, especially considering the challenges of frequent mechanical breakdowns, innumerable punctured tires, indecipherable foreign languages, intransigent government officials, and much more. Occasional problems faced by modern riders seem trite by comparison.

Two examples of vintage classics are: *Around The World on a Motorcycle: 1928-1936* by Zoltán Sulkowsky and *One Man Caravan* by Robert Edison Fulton, Jr. Both books are fascinating first-person accounts of around-the-world trips, the first beginning in 1928 and the second in 1932. Both are available in new printings from Whitehorse Press. Fortunately, the

The Blue Ridge Parkway ranks high on many bikers' list of the best rides in the country. Photo by John Cheetham.

~

A perfect waterproof match safe is made with an empty shotgun shell and a cork.

~

urge to record motorcycle adventures has not diminished over the decades. In fact, there has been a steady stream of published accounts, many available at your local library or favorite bookstore.

Riders need not go to the extreme of traveling around the world or deep into remote jungles to find excellent options for camping; a lot of prize-winning destinations are much closer to home.

One example of a fun and welcoming destination is the Blue Ridge and Smoky Mountains in the American mid-south. The fun part is the result of thousands of miles of twisty roads and gorgeous scenery while the welcoming aspect is due to the largest concentration of motorcycle campgrounds anywhere on earth. Riders by the thousands flock to this area each summer, some as day visitors, and others to stay much longer. Some find the motorcycle campgrounds perfect destinations while others use them merely as base camps while exploring the area. So whether the goal is to find a restful—and sometimes fun-filled—location to kick back and enjoy a few days' leisure or to ride the twisties to your heart's content, this area is unparalleled.

MOTORCYCLE RALLIES

Also deserving consideration here are motorcycle rallies as they are very worthy camping destinations. In fact we personally know hundreds of bikers who prefer rallies as their one and only destination. Not all rallies are as big as Daytona's Bike Week—but then, they don't have to be. Rallies are fun regardless of their size or where they're located, and if nothing else, they're great excuses for cross-country camping trips.

As popular as the big rallies at Daytona and Sturgis are, not all rallies follow that same format. There are rallies that cater to specific makes of bikes, rallies sponsored by motorcycle manufacturers, rallies for old bikes (or old riders), and rallies especially for Christians. The following is intended to be a sampling of the major rallies. There are many more listed in motorcycle periodicals and online.

DAYTONA BEACH BIKE WEEK AND BIKETOBERFEST

800-854-1234 · www.biketoberfest.org

By dint of sheer numbers Daytona Bike week is not only the largest of the rallies but the largest motorcycle event of any kind in the world. No one knows for sure how many attend the week-long event held every March, but estimates place the average attendance at more than one million. With that many bikers in town it's not surprising that every hotel room within a fifty-mile radius is booked at least a year in advance and that the commercial campgrounds are packed to capacity. In fact, so high is the demand for campsites that several temporary camping areas are opened each year just for Bike Week.

The biker's version of Mecca, Bike Week at Daytona Beach, Florida, is something every biker should experience at least once.
Photo by Jim Woofter

19

Daytona Beach Bike Week in March is one great way to combat cabin fever. Photo by Jim Woofter

~

A large wooden cigar box will make a swell box for fishing gear or anything else. Use the wood from a similar box and glue to make partitions in the first.

~

What's the big attraction of these two events? Consider this: warm temperatures; crystal-clear blue skies; customized motorcycles; beautiful women; sanctioned bike racing at Daytona speedway; the world's largest and longest party; and the ubiquitous, round-the-clock roar of bike motors. Need we say more?

STURGIS

605-642-8166 · www.sturgis.com

Sturgis is different. Located in the Black Hills of South Dakota, the breathtaking beauty of the surrounding mountains is justification alone for making the trip to this rally. The town is located at the geographic center of a huge hub with spokes that reach out to Mount Rushmore, Devils Tower National Monument, Custer State Park, Deadwood City, Wind Cave National Park, Badlands National Park, and much more. As if this weren't enough, bikers must ride across huge mountain ranges on all sides just to get there.

Like Daytona, the number of bikers attending Sturgis can't be known for sure but it's in excess of a half million bikers according to published reports. Also like Daytona, the predominantly Harley-Davidson-riding crowd quickly exhausts hotel capacities in a 50- to 100-mile radius. However, because there are significantly fewer hotels there than in Daytona, a larger percentage of attendees camp. Campers utilize the many permanent commercial facilities as well as temporary camping areas that operate each year during the rally. Travelers may find listings, photos, and contact information for all camps by searching on the Internet for "Sturgis camping."

Aside from the predominant brand of motorcycle and clothing in evidence at these three rallies, another factor they have in common is that participants are there to have fun. Usually loud, raucous—albeit, harmless—fun. With the exception of the Katmandu Campground, which promotes itself as "the quiet campground" and invites those who want to make noise to camp elsewhere, campers can probably look forward to the type of carefree partying that is unique to Harley riders at any of the other facilities.

Just say the word "Sturgis" to any biker on the planet and he'll probably know what you mean. Photo by Jim Woofter

The rallies listed below are as different from the Daytona and Sturgis rallies as night and day. The most obvious differences are that the motorcycles are quieter, their riders older, and that a greater percentage of the motorcycles are imported. There's also a joke among riders that these riders also spend more time at ice cream stands than bars. Actually, there's a lot of truth in that as most of this group never, ever, mix alcohol and motorcycles.

AMERICADE

518-798-7888 · www.tourexpo.com

Held each June in the town of Lake George, New York, Americade is one of the oldest rallies. This event, which includes a large motorcycle trade show, instructive seminars, and family entertainment, actually began as a Honda Gold Wing rally, but has since become brand neutral. The host city lies at the southernmost tip of its namesake, Lake George, in the beautiful Adirondack Mountains. The surrounding mountains provide outstanding riding in the area as well as many other attractions including wineries, the nearby Adirondack museum, the historically famous Fort Ticonderoga, Fort William Henry in the heart of the town and, of course, the lake itself with its fleet of magnificently restored passenger steamboats. The Adirondacks have been a favorite vacation get-away area since wealthy New York City moguls first discovered them a century ago. Indeed, when the golden era of camping and woodcraft first

The ice cream shops do a land office business in Lake George during Americade.

sprouted, most of its early roots were here. Remnants of that era are plentiful, with many magnificently restored homes and inns—many constructed with native logs. Rally-goers will find accommodations and campgrounds plentiful here and in nearby communities.

WING DING

800-843-9460 · www.gwrra.org

Speaking of Gold Wings, one of the largest brand-related motorcycle clubs in the world is the Gold Wing Road Riders Association. Started in 1977 by seven friends, the club now boasts more than 80,000 members in 53 countries! And there are more than 800 individual chapters. Members' benefits (Gold Wing or Honda ownership not required) include a monthly magazine, free emergency road service, chapter life, instant camaraderie with other members, district rallies, and a huge rally annually.

The "Wing Ding" national rally is held in early July in a different location each year. Recent rally sites have included Madison, Wisconsin; Tulsa, Oklahoma; Albuquerque, New Mexico; Greenville, South Carolina; Knoxville, Tennessee; Louisville, Kentucky; Billings, Montana; Huntsville, Alabama; and Fort Wayne, Indiana; all locations are able to support large numbers of attendees requiring motel/hotel accommodations as well as camping.

"Wingers" love camping. A sure sign that summer has arrived in the U.S. is the sight of Gold Wings on the Interstates towing their color-matched cargo or camping trailers while the rider and passenger sport their color-matched riding suits and helmets as well. An amazing sight pre- and post-rally time is the seemingly unending moving rainbow of motorcycles on every highway for hundreds of miles in every direction from the designated rally city. Of course the campgrounds present an awe-inspiring site of their own with equally colorful camping trailers and tents. The Dairy Queens along the routes are popular and busy.

BMW INTERNATIONAL RALLY

639-537-5511 · www.bmwmoa.org

Not to be outdone, the BMW Motorcycle Owners of America (BMWMOA), an international organization of predominantly, but not exclusively, owners of BMW bikes, also hosts, through its many chapters, regional rallies as well as a large International Rally each

~

If you plan to use horses or oxen to carry your camp, make sure your campsite has good grass.

~

The yearly BMW International Rally is held in a different location in North America each year. This one was in Trenton, Ontario, Canada.

year. There is one major difference between these rallies and the others. At BMW rallies the majority of attendees choose to camp. It may be, as some surmise, that campers prefer to buy BMW motorcycles, or that owning a BMW encourages camping, but whatever the impetus, all have discovered that camping has advantages and benefits that can't be ignored or equaled.

The BMW International Rally is open to members and non-members alike and, as with the others, features a large vendor show, demo rides, entertainment, seminars, giveaways, and camaraderie. Admittedly smaller than other rallies with an average attendance of only around 7,500, this rally is the jewel in the crown for motorcycle campers interested in exploring the rally option.

Many camping aficionados enjoy rallies so much they simply ride to a new one each weekend during the summer.

AMA VINTAGE MOTORCYCLE DAYS

614-856-1900 · www.amadirectlink.com

The American Motorcyclist Association (AMA) is the granddaddy of motorcycle clubs. Founded in 1924 it now has over 300,000 members and is the leading lobbyist for motorcycle interests in Washington, D.C. With a membership this large, Congress listens. The AMA is also the primary sanctioning organization of bike racing and bike events of all types.

Located near the AMA world headquarters in Pickerington, Ohio, Mid-Ohio Raceway plays host to the yearly AMA Vintage Days. Many motorcycle campers include this event in their list of favorite destinations as the event has ample space and comfort facilities for camping. Things to see and do include vintage bike races, a swap meet, demo rides, and an extensive exhibition of antique motorcycles.

Camping opportunities for Americade cover the range of options, from secluded, as in this state-run facility, to the ritzy commercial campgrounds.

Let's see, I'll need foreign currency, maps, guide books and, oh yeah, a motorcycle rental.

Ain't no big rigs here! Mooney's Hog Farm and Campground at Sturgis, South Dakota biker camp. Photo by Jim Woofter

Planning a Camping Trip

Once a destination has been determined, the next step is tackling the planning required to pull the trip off. Surprisingly, this stage of the process requires more time and effort than first imagined. But I've always found that the more time spent in planning a trip, the more likely the trip will be a success.

The process of planning any journey, including a motorcycle camping trip, is fundamentally a matter of analyzing your own needs, desires, and expectations and then making choices that support them. There is no right way or wrong way, only what works best for you and your machine.

Before charging out of the garage you must think about what you want to see, where you want to go, and how much time you'll have to do it. Are you constrained by time to "beat feet" to a specific destination, or does time allow a visit with Aunt Tilly in Cucamonga, and the luxury of avoiding four-lane slabs in favor of our beautiful two-lane "blue" highways? Are there specific camping places where you'd like to stay?

None of these questions are out of the ordinary; they're the same ones you must answer when traveling by car, but for motorcyclists there are a couple additional twists.

Test your daily riding range by taking practice rides with all your gear, increasing the distance each time until you find your limit. Photo by Brent Hartman

DETERMINING YOUR RIDING RANGE

Riders cannot plan a multi-day route without knowing how far they and any passengers can comfortably and safely ride in one day. It sounds simple enough but even a surprising number of experienced riders who are new to touring make the erroneous assumption they can ride as far on a bike in a day as they can in their cars.

Some bikers can't or simply don't want to ride as far on their bikes as in a car, while others seemingly have no limit. There is something to be said for taking your time cooking and eating breakfast, leisurely packing, and departing late—followed throughout the day with frequent rest stops, long lunches, and early quits. To many bikers this is the epitome of the good life and they wouldn't have it any other way. Only 250 miles per day . . . so what?

Then there are those who are up at the crack of dawn and ride until dark, spending little time off their bikes. For them 500 to 600 miles might be just an average day.

The point is that everyone is different. No one can tell you what your range should be and you should resist pressure, from yourself or others, to ride beyond your limits. Please don't forget the range of your passenger, if you have one, may be entirely different from yours.

There is no right or wrong, only what's best for you.

A safe and convenient way of determining range is by riding ever-increasing loop routes that begin and end at your home. This may take a few weekends but the advantage to this method is that you'll never ride beyond your limits and you'll never find yourself out on the road, either unable to return or away from lodging. Simply begin with a distance that you know from experience is doable and gradually increase it until the distance becomes uncomfortable. Even when you plan to return to your own bed, you should pack your bike completely with luggage and camping gear and ask your passenger to come along for the ride, as these things will have an effect on your overall mileage range. Don't forget to adjust your range to allow time at the end of each riding day for setting up camp and getting comfortable before night sets in. Yes, camps can be set up after dark, but it's never much fun.

~

You can avoid getting moonstruck (which is the same as sunstroke) by not sleeping with the moon shining on your face.

~

ROUTE PLANNING

With few exceptions such as Alaska or parts of the Far North of Canada, there's usually more than one way of getting from one point to another with no one able to say that one way is wrong and another right. It's pretty much a matter of individual taste as in the choice between interstate riding versus two-lane blue highways.

That said, there are three major requirements that must be borne in mind when outlining a route. The first is the availability of food and fuel stations. In urban areas riders hardly need to give this a second thought due to the proliferation of providers. On the other hand, there are many routes in certain areas where services are few and far between. In fact, they can be so scarce that riders can find themselves stranded without fuel. Secondly, there needs to be camping areas with available campsites along the route. (More on this below.) Finally, and equally important, riders must be aware of road conditions.

MAPS

There is just no substitute for good old-fashioned paper maps; a full-sized road map will be required for each state on the route. Maps are neat. Most riders who have done any traveling at all, by car or bike, will already have a collection of battered, well-marked souvenirs of trips past. A brand-new map is just about guaranteed to fuel the imagination with its wealth of possibilities. So where do you get new, up-to-date maps? Remember when gas stations pumped your gas,

~

Do not leave human waste exposed near your camp as it will attract bears and other wild animals.

~

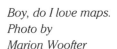

Boy, do I love maps.
Photo by
Marion Woofter

checked your oil, and gave away free maps? Well, those days are long gone. Maps are big business and big bucks today and so most service stations sell them for at least the state in which they are located. However, as the rider needs them before his trip for planning, there are alternative means of obtaining maps . . . and for free, too.

Both the American Automobile Association (AAA) and Canadian Automobile Association (CAA) offer free maps to their members. Because of their high level of detail and frequent updating, auto club maps are probably the best available. Another source of free maps are the states themselves. Every state and each Canadian province has a department of tourism that will be only too happy to send you a packet of information which includes the latest sightseeing and event information, as well as a road map. All you have to do is call them or contact their web site. Since there may be a few weeks delay between the time of your request and arrival of the packets, phone early. February or March is a good time. Be sure to specify your need for camping-related information, as this is frequently not included in the standard packets. For a complete list of contacts, see Travel Bureaus at the end of the book.

Atlases are not recommended for detailed route-finding but they are good in initial planning stages for deciding which states and major routes to follow. They're a lot easier to manipulate than large folding maps, particularly when lounging in an easy chair. Another plus for atlases is all the other travel related information included: lists of national parks and facilities, state-by-state road regulations, and charts for estimating traveling time.

An atlas is a good tool to use while deciding on the broad plan for your trip.

One unique variation is the *DeLorme Atlas & Gazetteer.* Are they atlases or are they map books? Produced in separate volumes—one for each state—they constitute a unique and inestimable library of information. Based on official U.S. government geological survey maps, each book contains unparalleled detail that is indispensable for exploring territory off the beaten path. For example, the Oregon edition divides the state into 72 individual 11 × 17-inch pages that, if cut out and fastened together, would create a state map of more than 86 square feet!

Though the size of atlases may make them impractical for some riders, others find the effort to be worthwhile. Excellent paperback atlases such as those by Rand McNally can be purchased at many discount and drugstores for around five dollars. The DeLorme atlases, usually found only at booksellers or online, are about $20 to $25. If you don't want to buy an atlas, the reference section of any library will have one or more hardbound versions you can use.

Mapping programs are amazingly accurate at calculating distances and travel times.

MAP READING 101

Shhhhhh, if you are one of those people intimidated by maps, we promise not to tell anyone, if you promise to read this. Here are a few tips that may help to de-mystify maps.

First off, maps aren't rocket science; in fact, they're amazingly simple. Really. First off, all commercially printed maps follow standard conventions and so, though they may cover different areas, they are still similar, and so making sense of them is a lot easier. Here's the first rule: all maps point north. That means when the map is opened up so that you can read it, the top of the map is pointed north—like to Canada or the North Pole. The left of the map points west to California. The right side of the map points east toward the Atlantic Ocean if you're in North America, or if in Europe farther east toward Moscow. That leaves the bottom of the map pointing to the south. Think South America, Africa, or the South Pole.

Maps usually have a legend or key—a box containing information about the different symbols used on the map, such as the different types of roads and the different sizes of towns and cities. Typically the legend will contain several small segments of differently colored lines indicating the relative size and importance of roads and highways. The thickest lines indicate the major multi-lane highways: interstates, motorways, and autobahns. A close examination of these lines will reveal that they are double lines rather than single, solid lines.

Next in decreasing order are multi-lane roads, which are usually limited to shorter distances within states, provinces, or municipalities. These symbols will usually be a different color than the interstate highways but will still be double-lined. Lastly, and represented by another color yet, are thin, solid lines representing local two-lane roads.

Cities and towns are often designated by circles ranging in size from small round dots to larger circles depending on their respective populations. The legend will give the population size ranges associated with each symbol. On the map itself, town sizes are also indicated by the size of the letters in their names. Names for larger cities will be spelled with larger, bolder letters than those used for small towns and communities.

There are a lot of numbers on maps but they too follow standard rules. Numbers superimposed directly onto roads indicate their own unique route number. These numbers, like license plate numbers on vehicles, are not duplicated anywhere else. For example, M5 is the main highway connecting Exeter with Birmingham, England, "The 400" (as it is known in Canada), is the major route between Toronto and Barre, Ontario, while Interstate 90 runs coast to coast through many large cities between Boston, Massachusetts, and Seattle, Washington, USA. In their respective countries these numbers are not used to designate any other roads.

Smaller numbers adjacent to, but not on the road lines, are distances, measured in either miles or kilometers, depending upon the system used in that country—the legend will say which—between towns to the left and right. They may be colored to coincide with the color of its road, but not always. These

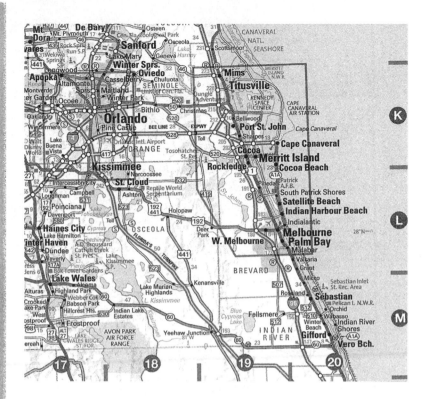

numbers are very accurate and can be relied upon when calculating distances.

Surrounding the map diagram on all four sides will be letters and numbers. On some maps the numbers may be found across the top and bottom while letters will be on the sides. On others this pattern may be reversed with no consequence.

Finding the location of a city can be done by using the index table located elsewhere on the map. Adjacent to each place name in the index is a letter and number corresponding to a matching letter and number found along the top and bottom and sides of the map. By tracing imaginary lines between like numbers and like letters the resultant intersection will designate a

small area in which the sought-after place is located. It works like this: Abbotsford, BC, Canada is given the index designation of Q-12 on the American Automobile Association (AAA) map of British Columbia. Tracing a line between the Qs at the left and right sides of the map and the 12s at the top and bottom yields the small area where, after a few seconds of searching, Abbotsford can be found.

It is recommended that the beginning map reader start with a map of his own state and, armed with the above tips, practice locating places, calculating distances, and tracing routes to familiar places. After a little practice, map reading and usage on a grander scale will be a snap. ■

Computer literate riders are probably asking, what about mapping programs? These programs are valuable resources but are not recommended for this stage of planning. Computerized mapping programs are easy to use and readily available. There are free versions on the Internet and other commercially available programs on CD are available almost anywhere software is sold. Prices start at a few bucks for the less frilly programs, but even the best, most comprehensive versions, such as Streets and Trips from Microsoft are only a few dollars more. These are extraordinarily detailed and capable of calculating mileage, mapping routes, estimating travel times, and a whole lot more. There are also free mapping programs offered by Internet service providers and some others in the public domain that merit consideration.

GETTING DOWN TO IT

As I mentioned above, atlases, because they offer a grander view of countries and individual states or provinces, are great for making those large-scale decisions, such as which states to traverse, the general direction of travel in each and perhaps which interstates, highways, or autobahns to use. Next, open up the full-sized state maps on a large table and begin penciling in the favored route. Do this for each state if there is more than one. Later, after the route is confirmed, the route should be remarked with a highlighter.

The next step—determining the daily distance—is more time-consuming but very important and is easier with the aid of a calculator. With a pencil jot down on a piece of paper the mileages indicated beginning with the starting point. (Writing each down allows accurate re-checking). Now add these together as you go and stop when you have reached your daily riding range limit. Finally, go back to the beginning and put a tiny mark along the route each time you reach 2/3

A good compass can be a life-saver … if you know how to use it.

Individual state paper maps are the best option for fine-tuning trip details.

The road conditions in construction zones can be downright hazardous fo motorcyclists. Try to locate them in advance of your trip so you can plan your route to avoid them.
Photo by Brent Hartman

of your fuel tank consumption. Now ask and answer these questions, is each gas tick mark near a location where fuel is available? Is the final mark near a location where camping is available? If the answer is yes, then this stage has been completed and the next, and each succeeding stage can be similarly done.

This process may appear unnecessarily regimented and contrary to the vagabonding spirit that is wistfully associated with the idea of motorcycle touring, but the realities of the modern road demand it. Unless the route is through very, very remote areas, the days are past when a biker can simply pull off the road at will and set up camp. Not only is this illegal most of the time and can result in a court citation or worse, it also exposes the camper to ever more prevalent predators—the two-legged kind. Additionally, since the season for motorcycle camping coincides with everyone else's holiday time, accommodations of all types are typically in short supply. Waiting until late in the day to find a campsite or a hotel room can be an exercise in futility. Thus, it's important to have a campsite reserved where and when it's needed. (More on finding a campground below).

It would be nice to assume that every road on the route would be in excellent or even passable condition but that just isn't going to happen. Cars and trucks can hop on just about any highway and make their way with little or no forethought to road conditions or construction zones. The worst that can happen is a delay in schedule or perhaps a detour. Not necessarily so with motorcycles. Summertime traffic tie-ups can cause overheating and other engine problems in air-cooled bikes. Additionally, traversing construction areas may require riding on scarfed surfaces—you know, those deep, wavy gouges cut into the old surface to give the new concrete or blacktop something to lock onto. Most bikers find this nerve racking. But worse yet are areas where the road surface has been completely re-

~

Always keep a spare paddle in your canoe.

~

35

moved, forcing bikes onto deeply rutted dirt, mud, or deep gravel—a challenge to all bikers and especially those laden with camping gear or towing trailers.

If hazards like these are likely to be a problem, you may want to consider using different routes or detouring around them. The trick is to know in advance where these areas are. Members of the American Automobile Association can obtain TripTiks®, custom-made maps outlining the best route to their destination and on which are high-lighted all reported construction areas as well as recommended detours. While these maps don't indicate what specific type of work or road surface conditions are present, they do indicate that something unusual can be expected. Also, many state police agencies have a phone number (sometimes toll free) that travelers can call to obtain road condition information.

Of course, one of the very best methods of obtaining the most up-to-date and detailed information is from other drivers who have recently traveled the same route. Internet-based clubs and organizations, chat lists, and discussion boards exist for just about every persuasion of motorcycling interest, and often a specific query about a certain route can elicit some very detailed responses from members who happen to live and commute in the area. And once you are underway, you can talk to truckers over a CB radio or in person at service areas and truck stops. Most will be glad to help, as are most other travelers you will meet on the road.

Now that the route has been tentatively laid out the only variable left to consider is any stops or visits you want to make on the way, for example if you needed to stop and visit an old school chum or if you wanted to allot a half day at Mt. Rushmore on your way to Yellow-stone National Park. Make sure to factor in more than enough time for variables such as these.

GPS

GPS technology has come a long way since the first edition of this book. GPS units are now more reliable, more accurate, more color-ful, and much, much less expensive—about one-quarter their earlier price. Another amazing development is their ability to give voice commands, such as when to turn and in what direction. This is ex-tremely useful when bike riders can't safely take their eyes off the

~

Trout will be scared off by your shadow cast on water.

~

road. Almost as prevalent as cell phones, these gadgets can be spotted sticking up from the handlebars on an ever-growing number of motorcycles. While a GPS should never be relied upon as a replacement for traditional maps, they can be a useful aid in other ways, such as locating sites within a strange city or finding food and fuel services while en route. Be forewarned, though, they should never be left unattended on a bike, as they are hot items for thieves.

COMPUTER MAPPING PROGRAMS

The strong suit of mapping programs such as Microsoft Streets and Trips is their ability to locate addresses, map routes, and generate GPS waypoints. For example, if a destination is located in a strange city or remote corner of another state, you can input the address and the program will not only display its exact location superimposed on a map, it can display detailed driving instructions. Many mapping programs can also calculate the waypoint's exact latitude and longitude, which can then be entered into a GPS unit. If the address isn't known but the location is, for example, Aunt Tilly's house on the corner of Elm and Maple, simply putting the cursor on the desired spot yields the latitude and longitude coordinates.

Mapping programs can also provide written instructions, which many travelers find useful. So detailed are they that they'll give turn-by-turn directions and even the exact distance as well as time required to travel on each individual road.

You may choose to print out your trip plans to carry with you, but, because most home printers are limited to standard 8 ½ -by-11-inch paper, there are a couple of problems. First, printing a complete route will require a sizable stack of pages and secondly, these are difficult to keep in manageable order.

GPS units are now as common as cell phones.

GPS NAVIGATION

For many motorists and motorcyclists alike, the must-have accessory for the last several years has been and still is a GPS unit. Many motorcycle manufacturers are including them as standard equipment. GPS units can be purchased just about anywhere and mounting brackets for motorcycles are readily available through most bike accessory catalogs.

In case you have yet to be initiated, GPS is short for Global Positioning System, which uses earth-orbiting satellites to pinpoint your location almost anywhere on the planet. But that's not all, as long as your unit is turned on, the system can monitor your every movement including direction, speed, and relationship to other points of known location. All of this means that if you are departing from home and want to visit Aunt Bessie in Tallahassee, the unit can communicate to you, via its small map screen as well as by spoken voice how to get there, where to make turns, how long it will take from any point en route to arrive, where to eat, where to get gas, and much more. GPS acolytes swear they will never be without one again. One of the neatest features is one which will automatically redirect you to the correct route as soon as it detects you've gone the wrong way. As if that weren't enough, available now are GPS units made especially with motorcyclists in mind. What sets them apart, aside from a higher price, are water-resistant cases and circuitry that allow them to operate in conjunction with Blue Tooth ear sets and helmet speakers. Of course that means that we'll finally be able to hear the GPS voice prompts but it also means we can access our phone books on the GPS screens as well as place and answer calls by touch commands.

The benefits of GPS units are many and proven, as are cell phones, but the traveler who is wise in the ways of the world knows that batteries can fail, screens can inexplicably go black, or heck, one might drop and break the thing in a parking lot. Additionally, as the new technologies as described above become more prevalent, let's hope the added distractions don't result in an increase in accidents.

Bottom line: use GPS at your own risk and don't leave your maps at home. ■

My favorite feature of the GPS is the accurate speedometer and odometer. I even discovered my bike speedo was five mph off!

Many campgrounds may offer no-frills camping cabins. By the way, no frills mean a bed and four walls. Photo courtesy of Blue Ridge Motorcycle Resort

CHOOSING A CAMPGROUND

While a few experienced motorcycle campers are quite happy roughing it in the wilderness, the majority of camping brothers and sisters prefer to do it with a few more niceties. They'll opt for one of the many, many full-service campgrounds scattered across North America and Europe. Selecting a commercial campground isn't any more complicated than choosing a motel or hotel, as you will be evaluating pretty much the same criteria: cost, location, and amenities.

Most travelers have limits as to how much they're willing to spend for a night's lodging, but this is rarely an issue for motorcycle campers, as sites for tents or pop-ups generally are the least expensive— $10 to 20 per night is typical at this time, although fees may be 25 to 100 percent higher if a site with utilities is required. Since there really are campgrounds that charge $75 and more per night, it doesn't hurt to check out the fees beforehand.

If "location, location, location," as someone once quipped, is everything for a business, it certainly is true for campgrounds. For riders keenly interested in getting from Point A to Point B in the least amount of time, the optimum camp location is as close as possible to their routes or destinations. For this reason, camps located at exits along major interstates are always packed to capacity during peak tourist season, as are camps located at or in the vicinity of major tourist venues such as Disney World or just about any national park. And for those seeking to avoid civilization, there are usually both commercial facilities and abundant opportunities for camping on remote public lands.

Sometimes amenities can play a significant role in your choice of campground, especially if you're planning to stay more than one night. At even the most basic commercial campgrounds you can usually expect to find hot showers and real toilets. More developed campgrounds feature game rooms, swimming pools, hot tubs, washers and dryers, canoe rentals, golf courses, camp stores, and much more. Some of these extras can be a welcome diversion after a hard day's ride or can even make the facility a dandy destination in itself.

Advanced planning and research will allow you to book campground reservations well ahead of your trip. Few travelers would dream of walking into a motel adjacent to a popular tourist site or thoroughfare in July and expect to get a room without a reservation. The same holds true for campgrounds during the busy summer season. Transient camps, those primarily servicing campers on the road, typically don't require as much advanced booking as others; often you can call in the afternoon to reserve a site for the same night. However, demand for spots at extremely popular destinations such as Yellowstone and Yosemite National Parks far outpaces supply, and sites are spoken for months in advance. The best advice is to do your itinerary planning well in advance of your trip and make any necessary reservations early.

So how do you find out where campgrounds are located and which ones to stay at? As always, there's no substitute for experience, so personal recommendations from friends or Internet newsgroup participants can be a gold mine of information. Other web sources are state and federal tourism sites and sites operated by the campgrounds themselves. But probably the most indispensable, all-inclusive and convenient resources are campground directories.

Camping directories are a camper's best friends for preplanning overnight stops or choosing a destination.

DIRECTORIES

Campground directories are compendiums of information on established campgrounds, listing everything from exactly how to get there to what their dates of operation are, with a description of facilities, services, and amenities. They'll also tell you what they charge for a night's stay and how to contact the facilities for reservations.

Three directories stand out for North American campgrounds: *AAA Campbooks, Woodall's Campground Directory,* and the *Trailer Life Directory.* The first, *AAA Campbooks,* are actually a regional series of thin, tankbag-sized guides that the American Automobile Association makes available free of charge to their membership. The latter two are much larger in size—about as big as a heavy phone book, as they cover all of North America and have paid advertisements in their publications. Rather than being a hindrance, the additional information in the ads (maps, area attractions, etc.) is very helpful in deciding which camp to use. Woodall's also offers several smaller, saddlebag-sized regional editions, which are less cumbersome to take with you on your trip. Most public libraries have Woodall's and sometimes other directories as well, although you may not be allowed to check them out. *Woodall's Campground Directory* is available for purchase through all booksellers as is the *Trailer Life Directory.*

Woodall's Campground Directory and *Trailer Life Directory* also follow an inspection and evaluation system. Woodall's notes that their maximum four-diamond rating does not necessarily equate to a "better" campground, as that judgment is most often determined by the individual camper's own tastes and values. More accurately, they state, the number of diamonds reflects the degree of camp development. Trailer Life Directory uses a numbered rating system, but the method is the same.

~

Pike fish are most certainly the outgrowth of water reeds.

~

All three directories use a similar format for conveying the data you would be looking for. A fictional listing for Bob's Fancy Camp might look something like this:

OHIO - Cortland

Bob's Fancy Camp Resort

From jct. Hwy 11 & SR 5 go $1/4$ mi. E on Hwy 5, then S on Ridge Rd. 1 $1/2$ mi., then W $1/4$ mi. on Bradlee Brownlee Rd. Entrance on right.

★★★★ FACILITIES: 102 sites, most common site width 35 feet, 50 full hookups, 30 water & elec. (30 & 50 amp receptacles), 20 pull-thrus, 22 tent sites, a/c allowed ($), cable TV hookups, heater allowed, tenting, dump station, laundry, playground, shower house, public phone, groceries, RV supplies, LP gas, ice, tables, fire rings, wood.

★★★★ RECREATION: rec room/area, Internet hook-ups, coin games, swimming pool, lake fishing, basketball, volleyball, planned activities (weekend only), hiking trails, horseback riding.

Open Memorial Day through Oct 15. Big rigs welcome. Rate $18-20 for 2 persons. MC/VISA. Phone (800) 555-CAMP.

Note that Bob's Fancy Camp Resort does not specifically exclude pets—or motorcycles, for that matter. If they did discriminate against two-wheelers, you might see the words "RV Only," which effectively excludes everything but motor homes and four-wheel towed trailers. Some campgrounds are more subtle with their motorcycle exclusion policies by simply specifying "No Tents." Though this is not very common, it is worth keeping an eye out for such things when perusing campground listings.

In addition to the campground directories cited, Coleman's has published the *National Forest Campground and Recreation Directory*, a compilation of—can you believe it?—4,600 different facilities in the United States Forest Service system! Some of the federal properties are covered in the previous directories, but if camping in National Forests is your bag, then this unique directory is the one you will want to consult. Another specialized resource worthy of mention is the saddlebag-sized *KOA Campground Directory*. KOA, short for Kampgrounds of America, operates more than 500 independently-owned campgrounds across North America. So prevalent are they that you could ride from coast to coast and never have to stay anywhere else. The KOA also operates an excellent website that has the same information as their published directory.

The famous miner tent is four sided and rises to a peak like a pyramid. The Sibley tent is similar to the Miner tent except it is round.

42

CAMPING IN EUROPE

There are many excellent resources that cover both European camping facilities in general as well as motorcycle-friendly camps in particular. European camping (frequently referred to as caravanning) is wildly popular, perhaps even more so per capita than in North America. Consequently, print and Internet directories are numerous. An excellent web site directory hosted by European Camping Guide; (www.europe-camping-guide.com) covers a whopping 6,000 facilities in 32 countries! For a web-based directory of motorcycle-friendly sites check out www.motobotc.co.uk/motocamp.htm. By the way, motorcycle camping in Europe is commonly known as moto-camping. A large selection of printed European camping directories is available from Amazon.com.

Non-Europeans who are interested in traveling to the UK or the continent will find it easy to rent motorcycles of just about any brand and size they prefer along with camping gear. A search for "European Motorcycle Rentals" on the Internet will yield an extensive listing of web sites operated by North American-based as well as European-based rental companies. Many also offer the option of group or solo riding, as well as conducted or self-directed tours.

~

Dig a deep garbage pit and cover each day's refuse with a layer of soil.

~

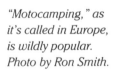

"Motocamping," as it's called in Europe, is wildly popular. Photo by Ron Smith.

~

Dead house flies dipped in melted paraffin wax make good fishing bait.

~

CAMPING IN U.S. NATIONAL FORESTS

Believe it or not, there are places where sleeping rough is allowed and even encouraged. They're called national forests (not to be confused with national parks). Scattered across America are millions of acres of public lands under the jurisdiction of the National Forest Service and these lands contain some of the most stunning geography to be found anywhere. A few well-known examples are the Bridger-Teton National Forest, Black Hills National Forest, Custer National Forest, Sequoia National Forest, Denali National Forest, and the White Mountain National Forest. All but a handful of states have national forests.

Locating these lands is not difficult; many are illustrated on road maps and atlases and the National Forest Service maintains a website that lists them all. In addition, some locations maintain their own websites that provide detailed maps, descriptions, and contact information. *Coleman's National Forest and Campground Directory* mentioned above is another good source of information, and one that you can tote on your bike. Don't let the title mislead you, even though some of these facilities may have traditional camping areas offering various levels of amenities including individual camp sites, toilets, and running water, many do not. And where they do, the campgrounds represent but a flyspeck on a vast area of undisturbed land. But the greatest thing is, you're not required to camp in the campgrounds; as a citizen this land is your land and you may camp anywhere you wish. The only restrictions are that camps must be at least 100 feet from lakes, rivers, streams, and roads, and you cannot

National Forests provide countless opportunities for camping.

occupy the same exact patch of ground for longer than 14 days. After that you may relocate your camp. No check-in or registration is necessary and there are no fees to pay. You are, however, required to respect any prohibitions on open fires that may be in effect. Otherwise, you're on your own.

Access to and through Forest Service lands is typically by a combination of paved and unpaved roads that bikers will have little trouble navigating. Many of the unpaved roads may have been used for old logging operations or for fire fighting. Rough camping on Forest Service lands is a wonderful experience. The opportunity to camp miles away from anyone else without a soul knowing where you are can be an incomparable occasion to enjoy the very best of America's outdoors. Additionally, with no pre-leveled, sanitized site awaiting, no convenient store around the corner, no water on tap, and no flush johnnies, camping on National Forest Service lands is a great test of camping skills.

AN ALTERNATIVE TO CAMPING

Many experienced campers have learned it's sometimes nice to be flexible—that an occasional break from a strict outdoor regimen to the comfort of a soft mattress and a hot shower is just the ticket for rejuvenating one's batteries. Sometimes, due to weather conditions or location, sleeping out is just plain impossible. Of course, you could always check into one of the ubiquitous motels that line the roadsides. A fantastic alternative, however, and one of the best-kept secrets of independent-minded travelers is hostelling.

~

Sharpened, short lengths of sticks will replace lost tent stakes very nicely.

~

"Hostel" is a Latin word for "inn," and just as the term is European, so too is the centuries-old tradition of offering wandering travelers safe haven in a roadside inn or a friendly farmer's barn. Just after the turn of the twentieth century, a German schoolteacher decided to organize many of these hostels into an organization benefitting the youth. A hundred years later, Hosteling International, formerly known as The International Youth Hostel Federation is the largest of a number of nonprofit organizations spanning the globe that offer safe, economical lodging to travelers of every age and nationality. In North America, this organization's facilities are operated under the auspices of Hosteling International USA (www.hiusa.org) and Hostelling International-Canada. (www.hihostels.ca)

Everything about hostels bespeaks their open-door policy for travelers, from the diversity of the guests and sleeping arrangements to the sharing of chores and modesty of their fees. Hostel guests are usually eclectic and always friendly—no averted eyes here. There may be hikers from every corner of the globe on hiking holidays, retirees, students, and even honeymooners. Sleeping arrangements can vary, but some hostels have private or semi-private rooms for couples and families, as well as open dormitories with shared living and kitchen spaces. Rules and fees vary too, but it's not unusual for guests to be expected to complete a chore or two before departing. At some hostels, you may not reserve a bed or room from night to night, but must leave by a certain hour in the morning and re-register in the afternoon. Did we mention that the prices just can't be beat? Many charge only around $20 dollars a night (as this book goes to press, a shared room at a hostel right in downtown Boston or New York city still costs less than $50). For additional information, a variety of excellent books are available at libraries, bookstores, and online.

NORTH AMERICAN MOTORCYCLE CAMPGROUNDS

So strong is the feeling of camaraderie among motorcycle campers that a few enterprising hosts have opened their own motorcycle-only campgrounds where you can indulge in your interests with other folks who are as passionate about motorcycling as you are.

Blue Ridge Motorcycle Campground boasts its own stream and great campsites.

Blue Ridge Motorcycle Campground
  59 Motorcycle Dr., US 276, Canton, NC 28716
  828-235-8350
  www.blueridgemotorcyclecamp.com

Comfort and conveniences are common at motorcycle campgrounds. Photo courtesy of Blue Ridge Motorcycle Resort

Deal's Gap Motorcycle Resort is smack dab at the bottom of the Dragon's Tail. This resort is where it's happening.

Deal's Gap Motorcycle Resort (a.k.a. Crossroads of Time)
US 129 & NC 28, HC 72 Box 1, Tapoco, NC 28771
800-889-5550
www.dealsgap.com
This is the place, the only place at the foot of the world-famous Dragon's Tail that winds upward through the rugged Smokey Mountains and across the Tennessee border to a high lookout some 11 miles and 318 white-knuckle turns later.

High Country Cycle Camp
765 Stony Fork Rd., Ferguson, NC 28624
336-973-7522
www.highcountrymotorcyclecamp.com

Iron Horse Motorcycle Lodge & Resort
1755 Lower Stecoah Road, Stecoah, NC 28771
828-479-3864
ironhorsenc.com

Iron Horse Motorcycle Lodge & Resort combines the spirit of the Old West with great facilities for relaxing in the mountains.

Paved drives and level campsites are welcome assets. Photo courtesy of Punkin Center Motorcycle Resort

Punkin Center Motorcycle Resort
 7304 Old Railroad Bed Road, Maryville, Tennessee 37801
 Main/Store: 865-856-5455
 Winter/Evening: 865-856-8877

Rider's Roost Motorcycle Resort and Campground
 100 Elk Creek Rd., Ferguson, NC 28624
 336-973-8405
 ww.ridersroost.com

Rider's Roost attracts huge crowds, especially those who ride Milwaukee iron.

29 Dreams Motorcycle Resort

53707 Hwy. 25, Vandiver, AL 35176
205-672-0309
www.29dreams.com

TWO Wheels Only Motorcycle Resort

P.O. Box 69 Suches, GA 30572
706-747-5151
www.twowheelsonly.com

Founded by Frank Chuk in 1983, this outstanding resort in the high Georgia mountains is now owned and operated by his daughter and son-in-law Brit and "G.T." Turner. Facilities include two campgrounds, swimming pool, airstrip, hot tub, gourmet restaurant, camping cabins, inn rooms to die for (in case you need a break from camping) and gracious hospitality. TWO is also a favorite weekend destination for motorcyclists from Atlanta and Europe. Yes, Europe.

Willville Motorcycle Camp

1510 Jeb Stuart Hwy., Meadows of Dan, VA 24120
540-952-CAMP
www.willvillebikecamp.com

If you enjoy wonderful camping, fresh water streams and a cool camp dog, Willville is the place to be.

There is nothing fancy at the Crazy Horse Campground—just unrestrained mayhem.

TEMPORARY CAMPS

Crazy Horse Campground
P.O. Box 357 - Rte. 16, North Bradley, WV 25818
1-888-GETCRAZY
www.daytonachamber.com/camping/index.htm
Camp located at 1425 Tomaka Farms Drive, Daytona Beach, Florida 32124

Daytona 200 Motorcycle Club
3602 Speedway Blvd., Daytona Beach, FL
386-252-2132
www.daytona200mc.com

New Smyrna Speedway Campground
115 N. Tomaka Farms Dr., New Smyrna Beach, FL 32170
386-427-4129
www.daytonachamber.com/nsscamp/index.htm

The Lot Next Door (next to The Cabbage Patch)
Corner of SR 415 & Pioneer Trail, Sarasota, FL
386-428-5459
www.daytonachamber.com/lotnext.htm ∎

The Rockies can give a scenic background to any snapshot.

The Mountain Laurel is abundant at Willville Motorcycle Campground.

The Camping Motorcycle

A popularly held notion is that a large, heavy bike such as the Harley-Davidson Electra Glide, Honda Gold Wing, or BMW K1200LT is required for serious road touring/camping. It's believed that these large heavy bikes are necessary to carry the large, heavy loads of camping gear. This is simply not so. In fact, an oddity of the motorcycle industry is that all bikes are designed to have roughly the same carrying capacity whether they are large, heavy machines or light, agile sport bikes. In short, this means that in all probability, a "small" bike can carry as much camping gear as a larger one!

Doubtful? Take a look at the numbers. The Gross Vehicle Weight Rating (GVWR) of the 2009 Honda Gold Wing is a whopping 1,338 pounds. Since the bike itself weighs 933 pounds wet, the difference between the two figures is its load carrying capacity of 405 pounds. Compare that to one of the nimblest sport bikes on the road, the Kawasaki Versys. It fairly tiptoes onto the scales at a mere wet weight of 452.5 pounds but with a GVWR of 851, its load-carrying capacity is 398.5 pounds—only 6.5 pounds less than the Wing! Why are their ratings so similar? It's because the manufacturers design the machines to carry two full-grown adults, approximately four hundred pounds.

Luxo-touring bikes are a popular way to camp, but not the only way.

~

A campfire that is kept
burning throughout
the night will consume
an entire tree of
cut wood.

~

Thus, to calculate any bike's weight-carrying capacity, start with its GVWR, which as required by law, may be found on a metal plate affixed to the frame of the bike. Subtract the bike's wet weight (with fuel and oil) from the GVWR. Now, to calculate how much gear the bike can carry, simply subtract the rider's weight, as well as the weight of any passenger from this last figure.

If the wet weight of the bike is not known, fill up with gas and oil and ride to a commercial truck scale such as those frequently found at truck stops, large farms, feed stores, or facilities that haul sand and gravel. Check trucking in the yellow pages.

It's never recommended that bikes be loaded beyond the limits that manufacturers have spent a lot of time and money ascertaining. Bear in mind they have no motivation in determining the ratings other than the safety of their customers.

Some riders believe that the weight capacity of bikes can be increased by adding more air pressure to tires or by increasing suspension spring pre-load. This is another false notion. Suspension spring pre-load can, indeed, on many bikes be increased but this is intended and allowed for. Factory settings are for nominal riding comfort and allowable adjustments for additional weight and comfort do not alter or increase capacity ratings.

Before setting out with a loaded motorcycle, adjust your suspension setting for the added weight. Photo by Kevin Dyer.

MAKING ADJUSTMENTS

Much more than automobiles, with their inherently stable four-wheeled design, motorcycles rely on their suspension systems for many of the desirable handling characteristics we seek. Fortunately, motorcycle manufacturers recognize the many uses to which our machines are put and have made it easy to make pre-load adjustments to both the rear shock (which usually bears most of the burden of an added load) and the front fork.

When the added weight of a load compresses the springs in the suspension system, there is less travel remaining to soak up the bumps in the road. Bikes vary considerably in the details, but in the simplest systems, a ramped or threaded collar located at the base of the shock can be rotated to further compress or expand the spring within. A spring that has been compressed will push back against its load with more force than before, effectively raising the back end of the bike and restoring some of the travel lost to the added weight.

While in use, springs by themselves may compress or expand more quickly than wanted, so modern forks (and some rear shocks) are enclosed in a sliding assembly filled with oil that damps these natural tendencies, slowing the rate at which it rebounds after a bump. Some motorcycles even use air pressure for fine adjustments.

Experienced riders have probably figured out which shock settings are best for unladen riding, and that's a good place to start. The owner's manual will have all the information needed to experiment further. Since safety and confidence will depend upon it, make the necessary adjustments to a bike's suspension well in advance of starting on a long trip to allow time to get used to the difference in the way the bike handles. Midway through a high-speed curve is not the time or place to discover handling problems.

Experienced riders like Larry Elliott of Cortland, Ohio, know that maintaining correct tire pressure is vital.

WHERE THE LOAD MEETS THE ROAD

Industry experts who offer free tire pressure checks at some of the major rallies report that the vast majority of touring motorcyclists they see are operating with significantly under-inflated tires.

As a tire rotates toward its contact patch, its shape flattens somewhat, only to round back out again as it continues to rotate away from the road. This constant flexing from roundness to flatness causes the underlying layers of crisscrossed synthetic cords to scissor back and forth against one another, creating heat, which is an enemy of long tire life. Under-inflation makes the problem worse by creating a larger contact patch, which flexes even more. It also causes mushy handling characteristics that are especially dangerous when cornering.

Over-inflation causes its own problems. Besides the obviously harsher ride, the resultant smaller contact patch actually causes a tire to wear quicker since the full force of the load is concentrated on a smaller area of rubber.

The appropriate air pressure for tires is given in your owner's manual, and that number should be the ultimate guide. Always check tire pressure when the tires are cold, as the heat generated by even a short ride will increase air pressure readings. Manufacturers have taken anticipated load- and heat-induced pressure increases into account when making cold-pressure recommendations.

To maximize tire life and ensure good handling, tire pressures should be checked often, preferably before every ride, with an accurately calibrated gauge. Invest in a quality model that can be used regularly. Warning: pencil-type gauges, the long thin type with the insert that travels in and out, are very inexpensive but also very unreliable. The best types are those with a round, glass-enclosed dial.

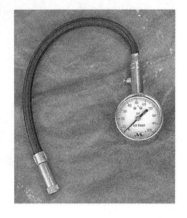

An air gauge with a flexible hose attached is ideal for reaching into tight spaces.

PRE-RIDE INSPECTION

Pre-ride inspections are well worth the effort. Riders have a responsibility to ensure that their bikes are safe and in good working order each time they're ridden. This is especially true when preparing for a camping trip considering the added gear and possibly a passenger to tax the machine. Riders may want to divide inspection duties into two categories: chassis and systems.

Begin the chassis inspection by going over the bike's frame inch by inch. Make sure there are no cracks, holes, or rust on any part of the tubing, welds, or brackets. Check all fasteners, such as screws, bolts, and nuts to make sure none are missing, stripped, or loose. Pay particular attention to engine mounts, luggage brackets, suspension components, forks, and handlebars. Speaking of forks, make sure the steering head travels freely from stop to stop and that the proper amount of damping is present in the forks.

~

Closed tents are damp, as they accumulate condensation.

~

Does the kickstand/centerstand work properly? If it doesn't retract as designed, replace the spring and clean and re-lube pivot points. At the same time make sure to inspect the welds that attach the mechanism to the frame. Then, spin both wheels by hand while eyeballing them closely to check for off-balance or out-of-round conditions. No free play should be present between the axle and hub while doing this. Finally, inspect tire tread for excessive or unbalanced wear.

The owner's manual will spell out the type, quantity, location, and frequency of replacement for all fluids used in the machine's various systems. If any fluids have exceeded or are close to exceeding their

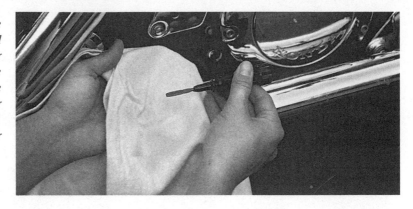

~

Two wool shirts are more useful than one heavy coat.

~

life, replace them as well as their respective filters. Inspect for leaks around all fluid reservoirs, lines, and fittings. Replace all hoses that are old or have weather cracks.

Hand- and foot-control systems should function freely and return to position when released, but check the owner's or service manual for cable lubrication recommendations all the same. Make sure all lever pivot pins and locking bolts are in position and secure. While checking the foot controls and linkages, it's also convenient to examine the drive chain or belt for wear and tension, if the bike has one.

The first component to check in the electrical system is the battery. If it's not a sealed battery, remove the top caps to see if the fluid is full, and if not, add distilled water. Battery-to-cable connections should be clean, as corrosion is a sign of power loss and likely an incomplete connection. If this is the case, disconnect the cables, clean the posts and cable connectors with a wire brush or emery cloth, and reattach. Use a voltmeter to test the battery for proper voltage and if low, either recharge or replace it. Lastly, inspect all lamp bulbs for proper functioning.

ROADSIDE ASSISTANCE

Some say there are two types of motorcyclists: those who have broken down and those who will. Of course no one can predict if, when, or where they'll break down, but of one thing you can be sure—instead of feeling helpless, bewildered, and abandoned when it does happen, it's comforting to know that assistance is but a phone call away, if you made the necessary arrangements before you left home.

Help is available from a variety of emergency road service (ERS) providers, often through popular travel organizations and associa-

Need a tow buddy? You can trust your bike with an unknown Good Samaritan or with a service authorized by a reputable Emergency Road Service plan. Photo by Jim Woofter

tions, such as the American Motorcyclists Association (AMA), Gold Wing Road Riders Association (GWRRA), Honda Rider's Club of America (HRCA), Harley Owner's Group (HOG), Good Sam Club, RV Roadhelp, and more. In addition, many motorcycle manufacturers provide emergency road service for a limited period as a free benefit with a new bike purchase.

By the way, don't overlook the company that provides your bike insurance, or the emergency service provider for your cars or other recreational vehicles. While many programs do not extend to motorcycles, some do and you might already be covered. As you might expect, not all ERS plans are equal. Fees, benefits, restrictions, and exclusions may vary from company to company. Here are a few things to keep in mind when shopping for coverage:

- Motorcycles require special handling. The only way to safely transport a motorcycle is on a flatbed car-hauler. Reputable emergency road service providers recognize the special needs of motorcyclists and require the towing services contracted to them to be so equipped. Be sure to verify this with the ERS of choice before signing up. And in the event that road service is needed, re-confirm that the towing service being sent out by the ERS to assist you will have a flatbed and tie-down straps. (Some bikers carry their own tie-down straps, just in case).

- If you will be towing a cargo or camping trailer, will your road service plan cover it? Be sure to ask before you sign on, as some will and some won't.

- Unless you enjoy the bureaucracy and hassle of filing for reimbursement on your claims, riders may want to avoid those companies that require you to pay all emergency expenses out of your own pocket, in favor of those who don't. Ask before signing up.

- Be aware of two types of mileage limitations that can affect overall satisfaction of a certain plan. The first, a minimum distance requirement, excludes all road service within a stated number of miles of the rider's home. (As extraordinary as this sounds, at least one ERS plan underwritten by the manufacturer of one of the most popular bikes in America has such a clause. If the breakdown occurs within fifty miles of home, there's no coverage!)

- The second, more common type of mileage restriction limits the number of miles your coverage will pay to haul you and the bike, typically stated something like this: "We will haul you and your disabled bike to the nearest repair facility that is capable of handling the repairs needed within one hundred miles." Other providers promise to tow the bike up to a preset dollar amount. Since terms of coverage vary so much between providers, make sure you know what you're buying.

- What kind of trip interruption coverage is included? If the breakdown occurs miles from home, does the plan pay hotel and food expenses? Will it pay, whole or in part, for a rental car? Many of the providers offer some form of trip interruption benefit at no additional cost.

HELPING HANDS

An alternative to seeking help from emergency road service providers is to seek assistance from fellow motorcyclists residing in the area of the breakdown or emergency. There are two prominent, brand-related, international networks of motorcycle owners who volunteer to offer assistance to fellow members in distress. The Gold Wing Road Riders Association (GWRRA) and the BMW Motorcycle Owners of

~

Never use a soldered pan or pot over an open campfire as the solder may melt and the item fall apart.

~

America (BMWMOA), each of which have thousands of members scattered across North America and Europe, have published tankbag-sized books containing the names and phone numbers arranged in alphabetical order by state and city of people willing to help. Each listing notes what sort of assistance each member can offer, from coffee and sympathy, to the use of tools and work space, to transporting a bike and providing emergency lodging.

In countless cases, these altruistic people who so generously make themselves available to other riders in need have made the difference between disaster and relief. What if the disabled bike isn't a BMW or a Gold Wing? No problem. As long as the rider is a member, help will still be offered. And don't despair of not being able to join one of these organizations because the bike is another brand, any motorcycle qualifies for membership and full benefits in the GWRRA. What's not to like?

EQUIPPING A CAMPING BIKE

Now that you're confident that your bike can carry all your gear, the question remains: how? The answer is by choosing the correct combination of luggage.

We've all seen bikes loaded down like two-wheeled versions of the Beverly Hillbillies' jalopy—with household accessories, kitchen

The gypsy look is neither cool nor safe.

gear, and drying laundry lashed atop a mound wrapped in a garbage bag that could be a sleeping bag. That's okay as long as nothing falls off! But experienced campers appreciate the value of keeping their gear reasonably organized and securely fastened to their motorcycles. Choosing the right luggage and knowing how to pack and secure it can have a direct and immediate effect on your health and welfare—a loose or shifting load can be a very dangerous thing on a motorcycle. In fact, the topic is so important that it's covered separately in Chapter 8: Packing Up. But choosing the right luggage will allow you to be organized. You'll be able to take everything necessary and will have no excuse for leaving critical gear at home.

You would have to look long and hard to find any motorcycle accessory that has gone through as dramatic an evolution as luggage. Beginning years ago with actual saddlebags from real horses, today's luggage selections encompass a wide array of materials, designs, and applications. Luggage may be made from aluminum, fabrics, plastics, fiberglass, and yes, even traditional leather, while taking the shape of saddlebags, trunks, tankbags, and more. Additionally, luggage may be built in—as a car's trunk is part of the overall body styling—or it may be attached to the machine's exterior. In any case, the whole gamut of options is available from aftermarket entrepreneurs (many of whom are experienced riders), as well as from an increasing number of motorcycle manufacturers.

SADDLEBAGS

Saddlebags have been around since the very beginning of biking, and so it's ironic that today's motorcycle manufacturers and aftermarket suppliers consider saddlebags to be one of the fastest growing new accessories on the market. In spite of all the contemporary hype, saddlebags offer some simple and time-tested advantages. They are easy to use, they provide a very secure method of carrying cargo, and most importantly, they enhance the stability of a motorcycle by carrying the cargo weight at the rear axle and near the bike's center of gravity. Every other method of carrying gear, to a greater or lesser degree, works against a bike's handling geometry by carrying the weight higher and farther away from the center of gravity. Since camping really does require you to carry a lot of gear, saddlebags should be the option of choice.

~

Bug guts, as small as they are, have tiny hard bits that can scratch your windshield if rubbed off. It's best to wait until early morning when nighttime dew has softened them for easy removal.

~

Fortunately, obtaining a pair of saddlebags has never been easier—they're as close as your nearest catalog, motorcycle accessory web site, or dealer's showroom, and you will have a myriad of types, features, and materials from which to choose.

LEATHER SADDLEBAGS

The original saddlebags were made of leather, and in the century since they were first used on motorbikes, the essential design has changed very little. Leather bags have the advantage of being tough and resilient, not to mention cool-looking. They can mold themselves around gear stuffed inside and they won't crack, shatter, or injure you if the bike goes over. Additionally, many brands are simply laid over the rear seat or fender and are just as easily removed for carrying. Many aftermarket leather bags are also significantly less expensive than hardbags.

On the downside, leather bags won't support your bike when it goes over, they don't have waterproof closures, and their contents must be wrapped in waterproof plastic bags so they won't get wet in the rain. And, since they cannot be locked, you may not be comfortable leaving your loaded bike unattended. Leather bags also have the unfortunate characteristic of sagging out of shape after continual use and old age (sounds like me). You can help prevent this by removing them from your bike when they are not in use and by being careful not to overload them. It's also a good idea to frequently give them a good drink of leather sealer or shoe polish. Not only will this help to keep the leather from drying out, it will also maintain a nice new-looking black sheen.

FABRIC SADDLEBAGS

Motorcycling isn't sissy stuff and soft luggage must be able to stand up to the elements and the rigors of the road. Fortunately, most reputable manufacturers in business today wouldn't dare risk their hard-

~

A fire starter can be made by shaving a dry stick, being careful to leave the shavings attached.

~

Fabric luggage is tough and resilient, even in the Andes. Photo courtesy of GIVI USA

~

An old Indian trick to slake thirst is to hold a small pebble in your mouth.

~

won reputations by using materials that are not up to the job. Which is why a heavyweight fabric, such as 1,000-denier Dupont Cordura, is a favorite. It will resist tearing and abrasion for many years of hard use. For protection from rain, luggage ideally should have either a removable cover or a lining treated with a water-resistant coating. Soft luggage typically attaches to the bike with a system of straps and either buckles or hook-and-loop fastenings. Strapping a large pack down securely will put a tremendous amount of strain on the system, so look for beefy components and reinforced stitching at stress points. For even more on the topic of gear construction and materials, see Chapter 5: Camping Gear.

Fabric saddlebags have all the advantages of their leather counterparts and even fewer disadvantages. Zipper closures can be locked and are therefore much more secure. Additionally, fabric can be constructed in a wider range of shapes than leather and it's easier to build in extra stowage pockets and compartments for organizing small things. Water-resistant fabric and generous zipper flaps will provide good protection in light weather conditions, but untaped seams should not be considered completely waterproof without additional treatment. Some fabric saddlebags come with additional rain covers for extra insurance. Like leather, fabric bags require some minor maintenance to keep them weather worthy. The best fabric saddlebags have integral support or are otherwise designed to minimize sagging loads, and often come complete with retro-reflective panels or strips to enhance your overall conspicuity in traffic.

Many believe the snazziest looking bags and trunks are those integrated into bike designs.

INTEGRAL HARDBAGS

Integral hardbags are those bags that are integrated into the body styling of the motorcycle, so from the standpoint of options, they're not. They're by far the slickest looking bags. Fit and finish are obviously superior, as are their locking mechanisms and waterproof seals. But every item has to have a downside and so, unfortunately, do some of these. A very important asset for campers is capacity and some bags just don't have much. (The bag should be large enough to hold a full-face helmet.) One reason why some bags can't carry even a modest volume of gear is that the backs of the bags are often cut in to provide clearance for the bike's shocks and other components. Appearances can be deceiving, so if bag capacity is important to you, inspect them closely, preferably with a full-faced helmet in hand. Also take note of the weight-carrying capacities of stock dresser bags; many manufacturers impose severe weight limits on their saddlebags. One last drawback is the lack of exterior storage surfaces. When stowage space really becomes a high priority, as when you are traveling two-up, small, soft packs are commonly secured to the tops and/or fronts of hard bags. Of course, you need flat, rather than highly stylized surfaces on your luggage for this to be a practical option and many of these bags just don't have any.

BOLT-ON HARDBAGS

There are three categories of bolt-on hardbags: stylized plastic or fiberglass, non-stylized plastic, and aluminum. Stylized plastic or fiberglass bags are the ones we've come to know so well on the large

~

To relieve a cough soak a pound of black cherry inner bark in a gallon of water for 24 hours then boil down to one pint. Take one tablespoon three or four times a day.

~

Where add-on luggage is mandatory, there's none stronger and roomier than those sported by these two bikes in South America. Photo courtesy of GIVI USA.

dressers and now are appearing on some cruisers as well. They are pretty to look at, boasting superb matching paint, or leather cladding, heavy-duty hinges and locks, and rain seals. And they do have top surfaces that may support additional soft luggage. Though these bags represent the fastest-growing segment of the saddlebag market, they are really not intended for camping, as their capacities are often exceedingly small. However, when packed judiciously and used in conjunction with other luggage, they can be useful.

For bolt-on bags with plenty of space, check out non-stylized hardbags from GIVI, an Italian manufacturer who offers saddlebags and tail trunks with capacities ranging from medium to gigantic (55 liter/bag). Though the bags themselves are generically designed to fit all bikes, the mounting brackets are customized for specific motorcycles. A terrific asset of these bags is their ingenious docking mechanism, which allows the bags to be detached and carried away like

Expert rider and craftsman Rod Sanlo of Ohio has equipped his BMW GS with large aluminum saddle boxes, and a self-made combination luggage rack. and security box. Note the smart use of straps to secure the heavy-duty dry bag instead of elastic cords. Photo by Rod Sanlo.

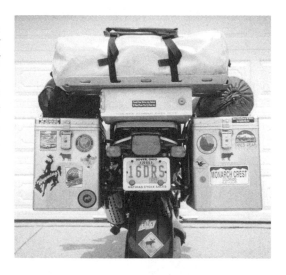

suitcases. Finally, their good looks, design, and functionality can be-lie their price, which can be half the cost of some bags offered by bike manufacturers.

Utilitarian bags made of aluminum make no pretense of being at-tractive, though they do have a homely panache which speaks of treks through deserts, jungles, and across mountain ranges. These bags are meant to carry a lot of gear and that they do well, passing the helmet test with flying colors. Aluminum saddlebags also have weather seals, locks, and flat surfaces on which to lash gear and stick travel decals. These bags do everything except shout, "Serious rider here!" Be warned, however, that aluminum saddlebags are not cheap and you should brace yourself for the sticker shock.

SADDLEBAG AND TRUNK LINERS

Liners are lifesavers and once you use them you'll wonder how you ever got along without them. And because they're fabric and custom made to fit the interior of your saddlebags or tail trunk, they take up none of your precious interior volume.

Their main function is to keep all your stuff from sloshing around in-side your cases. No more rooting around through a mess of everything to find what you're looking for, and no more spilling bits and pieces on the ground as the cases are opened or closed. With liners all the pre- and post-trip packing and unpacking can be done on a bed or table at home in an orderly manner. And because the liners have zippered panels that open to reveal the whole interior, finding stuff in the com-fort of a tent or picnic table is a breeze. Upon arriving at a campsite,

~

Night-time stuffy nose can be relieved by wetting the inside and outside of the nose with cold water and propping the head up on a pillow.

~

Form-fitting luggage liners are a blessing when it comes to packing and unpacking. They also keep everything neat and prevent rattling.

the liners can be lifted out and stowed in a tent or under the vestibule fly and just as quickly returned to the bike when leaving.

The bad news is that because liners aren't universally available for all sizes and brands of hard bags and tail trunks, finding them for a particular saddlebag or tail trunk can be a challenge. A search through motorcycle accessory dealers' catalogs will typically reveal liners for some brands, but not all. Some aftermarket luggage manufacturers have begun offering them as well and, of course, Internet searches will also be helpful. When all else fails, make your own. It's not rocket science, just heavy-duty fabric and zippers. Any boat cover or awning maker can whip out a set in no time as can any tailor or seamstress.

TANKBAGS

Serious touring riders have a thing for tankbags. Once someone has one, they're hooked and won't ever be without one. Like a wallet or a favorite purse, tankbags become repositories for personal treasures, necessities, and goodies we need and accumulate while traveling, things like sunglasses, cell phones, note pads, pens and pencils, matches, napkins, maps, toll change, cameras, extra film, and much more. Tankbags are also great places to stow the various pieces of clothing you'll add and remove as the temperatures change during a typical day's ride. It's handier than rooting through rear luggage. And any tankbag worth its salt will have a clear plastic pocket on its upper surface for holding maps. But beware, some map pockets may be too small to accept two sections of map laid open ($9 \times 7 \frac{1}{2}$ inches), and the maps will have to be scrunched in.

~

You can lengthen your life by never breathing through your mouth.

~

Tank bags have a long list of assets, but remember only use the main compartment for soft items like clothing. In the event of an emergency stop hard stuff like cameras or lanterns can break bones.

Check out the dimensions of the map pocket before buying a tank bag. Many are too small to hold an un-scrunched map. Ideally the pocket will be at least 7 5/8 inches wide by 8 1/2 inches high.

Many long-distance riders claim that a nice tall tankbag stuffed with soft items makes an excellent pillow-like support onto which they can lean on to stretch and rest their backs for short spells on straightforward, undemanding roads. Of course, you should never sacrifice control for comfort, but it is amazing how much relief you can get by just being able to change your position in the saddle regularly.

Tankbags are available in a wide range of shapes and sizes, from tiny flat ones that hold nothing more than a map, to tall jumbo sizes. The best tankbags are made of heavy denier nylon and now are being offered in colors other than black. Numerous models are expandable, with the ability to grow as more stuff is, well, stuffed inside. These types begin with one compartment and have either one or two additional levels that may be revealed as perimeter zippers are opened. As an added protection against water leakage, some tankbags come with a rain cover.

Tankbags are attached to bikes with either straps or magnets. Note that gas tanks made of aluminum are non-magnetic. It is less convenient to attach and remove a strap-on bag (and remember, you must do this at every gas stop), whereas a magnetic bag is on and off in a flash. On the other hand, an opportunistic thief could walk off with a magnetic bag and all its contents in a heartbeat if you should leave it unattended. Because of this, many magnetic bag manufacturers do offer auxiliary tie-down straps to both prevent theft and curtail movement caused by road vibration.

~

A person lost in the woods may die of fear within an hour.

~

TANKBAG CHECKLIST

- ☐ Change for tolls
- ☐ Maps and camping directories
- ☐ Personal address book
- ☐ Notebook, pens, and markers
- ☐ Sunglasses
- ☐ Spare prescription glasses
- ☐ Medications
- ☐ Lip balm
- ☐ Antacid tablets
- ☐ Insect repellant
- ☐ Sunscreen
- ☐ Toilet paper, napkins
- ☐ Spare batteries and film for camera
- ☐ Cell phone with DC adapter and batteries
- ☐ Hat for covering helmet hair
- ☐ Spare gloves
- ☐ Extra set of earplugs
- ☐ First aid kit
- ☐ Sweater ■

If you use a tankbag, remember to keep the number of hard items stored in the center compartment to a minimum. Avoid large items such as tools, tent pegs, large cameras, or lenses inside your tankbag, as these things could injure you badly if you stopped suddenly. Also note that dirt and grit trapped under a tankbag can mar or even scratch your paint's finish. Take meticulous care in keeping both the bottom of the tankbag pad and the top of the tank clean. A very nice feature that more tank bag makers should incorporate in their designs is a small compartment at the end closest to the rider. This is an ideal place to keep toll road tickets as well as toll money.

PANNIERS

Pannier is the French word for bread basket (pronounced *pan-yea*). It is not difficult to imagine a Parisian peddling a bicycle toward

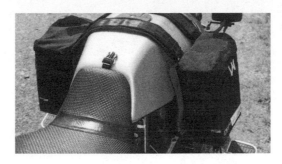

Regardless of how you pronounce their name, panniers are an ideal place to carry heavy, dense items such as cook stoves, fuel, food, and utensils.

home on a cobblestone street with the long ends of baked bread sticking upwards from the baskets hanging on either side of the front wheel. It's a romantic—and factual—image that is probably as realistic today as it has been over the last hundred or so years, especially if we see the rider sporting a beret. In any event, panniers have long been an excellent method of carrying stuff on bicycles.

Somewhere along the line innovative tinkerers adapted them to motorcycles and they are now an oft-used bit of luggage, albeit slung over gas tanks rather than front wheels.

Though some people use the term panniers when referring to saddlebags, they are not the same. Saddlebags sit behind the rider and over the rear wheel while panniers are attached in front of the rider.

Since panniers reside at or below seat level, they assist in stabilizing the bike by keeping the center of gravity low. A well-engineered pair can usually hold as much or more than one large saddlebag. Tank panniers will also provide some additional protection to your knees and legs in inclement weather. As with all fabric bags, the exteriors should be treated with waterproofing spray and the contents sealed in waterproof, zip-lock bags. One disadvantage of panniers is the restriction of airflow. For the same reason that panniers provide protection for legs and knees during cold or inclement weather, they may impede airflow forcing additional heat onto the rider. However, this is not always the case as different bikes have different air flow characteristics. It's recommended that riders try out a set of panniers before buying.

Because the market for panniers, like that for bag liners, is small, finding them may be equally challenging. It will be a rare motorcycle dealer that stocks them. However, as their use catches on they may become somewhat easier to find. Three sources are Touratech, Whitehorse Gear, and Campmor.

~

A few small tools, nails and boards for making camp furniture should be taken to your camp.

~

FORK ROLLS

When storage space is at a premium and every cubic inch counts, don't forget about fork rolls. Since they can only be used on bikes with fully-exposed forks, many bikes don't really have the option. For the rest of us though, fork rolls are a convenient place to stow tools, windshield cleaner, or a first aid kit. Fork rolls of black leather are readily available from cruiser accessory vendors, though more constructed of heavy denier nylon are appearing in the marketplace. Before buying a fork roll, make sure there is enough room for one above the highest level of fork travel.

TRUNKS

For years trunks tended to be associated only with large touring bikes. Now, thanks both to original equipment manufacturers and aftermarket suppliers, they are available for virtually every motorcycle. But don't expect to see the same gleaming, chrome-bespeckled affairs filling the aftermarket accessory catalogs. The newest genre of accessory trunks is less concerned with appearance than they are with utility. While not every trunk will fit every bike, every bike will have options available.

There's many a passenger who loves a hard trunk. Some trunks, like this one, even have built-in stereo speakers.

Italian-made GIVI, pronounced gee (as in gee wiz)-vee, hard trunks are specially designed for just about every motorcycle. They're superbly engineered, well-built, and all but bulletproof.

Hard trunks supplied as original equipment on full-dress touring machines have long been recognized for their rock-solid mountings, high strength, built-in keyed locks, interior lights, excellent fit and finish, and large carrying capacities. Most are large enough to hold two full-face helmets and, with the addition of optional luggage racks, can carry gear on their top surfaces as well. The only drawback is their cost. As you might expect, these goodies are expensive.

With the proper brackets, aftermarket hard trunks are available for just about any bike—good news for owners of sport, dual-sport, and standard bikes who want to significantly up their gear-carrying capacity for camping trips yet retain the advantages of theft and weather protection. As with saddlebags, the aftermarket leader for bolt-on hard trunks is GIVI.

For riders who place a priority on leather styling, rigid leather travel packs from Harley-Davidson and other aftermarket makers may be the trunks of choice. These attractive, spacious trunks are made from thick, high-quality leather that is treated to retain its shape and resist the effects of weather. Typical designs can be cylindrical, rectangular, or square. Rigid leather trunks can be adapted to many different bikes and should last a long time with proper care. Riders are cautioned against carrying additional gear on top of leather trunks, as it can distort or damage them. Users must also be aware that these bags are not watertight and their contents should be sealed in waterproof containers.

~

Canvas relaxes and sags when wet. When this happens you must be prepared to go outside and tighten all the guylines to keep the fabric tight.

~

*Tailpacks come in all
sizes from tiny...*

...to humongous.

*For solo campers
they're indispensable.*

TAILPACKS

Imagine duffel bags that have been fed a sugar diet, shot up with steroids then morphed with Hollywood special effects. If you can do that then you've got a pretty good idea of the variety of motorcycle tailpacks available today. In size, they range in capacity from two sandwiches and a banana all the way up to a side of beef. Configurations vary as well. Some are meant to lie down, others to stand up, and still others do both. Shapes? You have your choice of rectangular, square, cylindrical, or horseshoe. In short, there's something for everyone, so it's no surprise that tailpacks have become one of the most popular types of luggage used by motorcycle campers today.

The earliest tailpacks date back to the time when hard trunks and voluminous saddlebags were the sole province of only the largest bikes. Tailpacks offered promise to smaller bikes that they too could haul a lot of gear. When compared to hard luggage, tailpacks are usually quite an economical option, and they can be quickly detached and easily stored between uses. When positioned directly behind a rider, a well-secured tailpack should disturb a bike's handling very little. Soft-sided bags also conform well to the oddly shaped gear one hauls on a camping trip, and fabric designs can incorporate extra compartments and storage pockets that are very handy for keeping things organized.

Tailpacks require no special mounting brackets or hardware and often fit a wide variety of bikes. As with all luggage, you should ensure that the combination of straps, buckles, and/or hook-and-loop fastenings responsible for keeping your pack secure are beefy enough to do the job, and fixed to the pack with reinforced stitching.

~

A hunting horn
is useful for calling
others to dinner
or to those lost
in the woods.

~

Tri-Bag systems are the newest derivation of soft luggage. Tail pack and saddlebags work as one. This is a great asset for bike stability and safety.

Smaller bags sometimes attach to a motorcycle with built-in elastic cords; this method is certainly not recommended as the sole means of attaching larger packs. Note that the end-hooks on the cords can irreparably scratch your paint as well. For more on the important topic of securing luggage, see Chapter 8: Packing Up.

While the largest-capacity tailpacks are typically configured to lie low and across the rear seat, some bags are made to stand up vertically behind the rider, supported by a sissy bar. When packed with soft items, riders can even lean against these packs for some welcome back support. The manufacturer most associated with this type of design is T-Bags of Santa Ana, California, though there are additional makers. While tail packs are especially popular with the cruiser market, they can be adapted to just about any motorcycle with a modest sissy bar or hard trunk. As a bonus, many of these packs come with shoulder straps and can serve double duty as backpacks.

~

15 to 20 yards of half-inch rope is useful in a camp.

~

DRYBAGS

One of the slickest ways to carry a lot of gear on your motorcycle is in a dry bag. At first glance, their simple, army-surplus duffel bag styling might not catch your eye, but you should be prepared to take a second look. Dry bags are durable, less expensive than hard saddlebags and tail trunks and—most importantly—100 percent waterproof, even when fully submersed.

Dry bags, like this one from SealLine were actually designed for boaters, especially rafters, kayakers, and canoeists where gear is constantly exposed to water. The largest, like my own zip duffle, holds a whopping 75 liters. That's way more than any hard trunk.

Drybags may be made of an outer layer of heavy nylon fabric coated with durable PVC or urethane joined with seams that have been taped against moisture. Others consist of a very thick outer layer of PVC bonded to a fabric interior. Seams are sonically welded for maximum strength and waterproofing. Dry bags come in a wide variety of sizes and configurations, right up to the truly huge; at 76 and 80 liters plus, each of the two largest SealLine duffels actually has more capacity than a hard trunk! The longer versions may be too wide to get adequate support when laid crosswise over the average seat or rack, so many bikers use custom-made racks. Another option is to use the saddlebags to hold up the ends of the drybag.

Zippered dry bags are very convenient, especially those with zippers that run diagonally from end to end across the entire length of the bag. These allow instant access to the entire contents of the bag.

Other dry bags use a roll-down closure that cinches to the bag. When this type of opening is located at the top of a tall duffel, it can be hard to get to items near the bottom of the bag without unpacking everything. This problem is tackled in some bags by incorporating see-through side windows, while in others the roll-down closure is located lengthwise along the bag.

KNAPSACKS, ETC.

Long popular in Europe, a small backpack is a dandy way to carry lightweight, low-volume items, such as a change of clothing, a jacket, or lunch without having to mess about upon arriving at your destination. If you know you'll be spending some extended time off your motorcycle, you can pre-pack your day bag before you leave camp, so that when you arrive you can just park your bike and run. And, it's just the thing for taking on a short hike or shopping trip, too.

~

A Dutch oven of heavy cast-iron is very useful for cooking.

~

Wearing a backpack while on a motorcycle may have a certain movie panache, but it really is a poor way of carrying anything when any other option is available.
Photo by Marion Woofter

As practical as many riders find them, though, backpacks aren't used as a primary method for hauling gear. There are too many other ways of packing up your bike that carry the weight more safely and comfortably. However, a small collapsible pack serves well when you are laying in food and supplies to take back to your campsite for the night, especially when your bags are otherwise full. No trying to bungee a slippery bag of awkwardly shaped items on top of your pile of gear. No crushing your loaf of bread or bag of chips by squeezing it into your top case.

Some motorcycle campers utilize a small cooler for perishable foodstuffs when on the road, strapping it to the rear seat, trunk top, or sissy bar. Even those riders who don't routinely cook when they camp claim it's a great way to keep beverages cool, so you can enjoy them when you want, rather than always taking your rest breaks in gas station parking lots where you bought your refreshment. Reusable ice packs aren't very practical when you are on the road for several days, as it is difficult to find the means to keep them frozen, but ice usually is available at most convenience stores.

~

It's always a good idea to take along your personal cook and manservant from home when camping.

~

TOOL KITS

Being stranded along a highway is always an unpleasant and frustrating experience—doubly so when it's for something that is easily and quickly repairable, like a missing nut, a burnt-out fuse, or even a punctured tire. While it's true that you may be one of the lucky few who never break down, odds are it will happen sooner or later. When it does, it's nice to know you can be up and running in short order thanks to your portable tool kit. Don't have one? Better get with the program and put one together—it could be the cheapest emergency roadside insurance you'll ever buy. If you do get caught out without a tool kit, however, or if you're in a jam for a 1/2-inch, left-hand widget, remember that most RVers carry substantial tool kits and are usually eager to lend a hand to a traveler in distress.

TOOL KIT

The contents of one's road tool kit can be a rather personal matter, but many of the items are pretty standard. A lot of riders (like me) carry more than we need in the event we come across a fellow biker who needs help. A few extra tools don't take up all that much more room, and besides, it gives you a warm, fuzzy feeling to help a guy get back on the road. Here's what you will find in my tool kit:

- ☐ Pencil and note pad
- ☐ Set of English and metric hex wrenches
- ☐ Set of English and metric box-end or combo. wrenches
- ☐ 3/8-inch drive socket wrench, with extension
- ☐ Socket, sized for spark plugs
- ☐ Screwdriver/nut driver kit with flat and Phillips tips
- ☐ Long-nose pliers
- ☐ Medium crescent wrench
- ☐ Pocketknife
- ☐ Headlamp or small flashlight
- ☐ Cable or disk lock
- ☐ Jumper cables (compact, in zippered pouch)
- ☐ Black electrical tape
- ☐ Duct tape
- ☐ Plastic cable ties
- ☐ Tiny plastic tube of WD 40 lubricant or similar product
- ☐ Voltmeter
- ☐ Spanner wrench for shocks
- ☐ Air pressure gauge
- ☐ Tire irons (optional)
- ☐ Tire repair kit (optional)
- ☐ 12-volt air pump or CO_2 cartridges

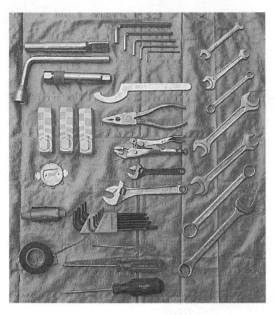

You can buy a kit (less money) or build your own (more money) like I did. This is most of what is in my everyday kit.

In addition to tools, I carry a few spare parts that might come in handy for my bike. If you have a chain-driven bike, it's a good idea to carry one or two spare master links. If you're really going out in the boondocks, consider taking spare brake and clutch cables.

- ☐ Spark plugs
- ☐ Spare nuts, bolts, washers, electrical terminals
- ☐ Fuses
- ☐ Bulbs for headlight, taillights, and brakes
- ☐ Electrical cable—6 inch × 16 gauge.
- ☐ Fuel filter
- ☐ Extra ignition and luggage keys ■

The whole tool kit fits in this padded and zippered case that was sold as a lunch tote at a discount store.

Not all campgrounds are crowded with RVs!
Photo by Cindy Sokoloff.

The presence of vendors' tents is a sign of a
well-run rally, big or small. Photo by Ron Smith

Camping Gear

Getting started in any new recreational activity usually involves a commitment to obtain specialized equipment. A quick spin through a motorcycle campground will reveal many pieces of unique and expensive gear. Fortunately, you can get started quite nicely without spending a lot of money. There is a wide selection of gear available to choose from, and it's likely that you may even have some old stuff of your own gathering dust in a family closet somewhere. Before you spend a lot of money, you might try using what gear you've got on hand, or borrowing gear from camping enthusiast friends. The latter has the added bonus of giving you some exposure to lots of different things before you have to decide for yourself. Also many outfitters rent gear and you might explore that option in the beginning.

Most camping gear sold today is aimed either at the recreational market or the backpacking crowd. Recreational campers typically travel by car or RV, so the weight and packed size of their gear isn't of great concern. Retailers also expect that folks in this category will probably not be camping under very extreme circumstances, so they may not need all the pricey features their more extreme brethren couldn't live without. If you are not cramped for carrying capacity, you may find very adequate entry-level gear at any of the big-box discount stores. A typical Wal-Mart usually has a nice selection of tents, cookware, and lanterns—everything you need. You may be able to improve upon any shortcomings of your gear by doing such things as rigging extra poly-tarps as ground cloths or as canopies.

At the other end of the market, muscle-powered campers (cyclists and hikers) place their highest priorities on gear that weighs as little as possible and packs very small. Because they often must rely on their gear completely for long periods in which they may have no other alternatives and under conditions that may be less than ideal, they value practical designs and bombproof construction. Motorcycle campers will find lots of things of interest in this category, as the carrying capacity of bikes have similar limits on volume and weight, but there is really

Shopping for camping gear is fun . . . and challenging.

BMW Motorcycle rallies always present a veritable sea of gear options to inspect. Photo by Ron Smith

~

Khaki-colored canvas duck tents have been found by the British as well as the U.S. government to be superior in every way to tents of other colors.

~

no need to go overboard. While it may be neat to have the very best and most expensive stuff going, it usually isn't necessary.

Once you discover that motorcycle camping is the greatest thing since the invention of the electric starter, you'll need to evaluate how well your tent, sleeping bag, and ground pad or cot do their job, as these are the items that will have the greatest influence on your camping experiences. You can then start to accumulate stacks of mail-order catalogs, spend weeks surfing websites, and drive your outdoor equipment store clerks nuts with persistent window shopping! This chapter should help you wade through the promos and sales speak, evaluate which features and benefits will be most important to you, and make confident, informed purchasing decisions when the time comes.

DECIPHERING THE LINGO

Speaking of sales speak . . . product labels and catalog descriptions of gear use a language all their own. When your hard-earned dollars are at stake, it helps to start off with a working knowledge of the terminology manufacturers use to describe the common features of their products. Short of that, a novice consumer will tend to make choices based on something he can relate to: price. Unfortunately, he may find out, too late, that his "bargain" finds were actually expensive mistakes in the long run. Like most things in life, you do tend to get what you pay for, and the details of construction and materials will often correlate directly to a higher or lower price point.

When you see a particular fabric described in ounces, the figure refers to the weight of one square yard of material; in general, the higher the number, the tougher and longer-lasting the fabric. The denier of a particular thread is the weight, measured in grams, of a single strand 9,000 meters (5.59 miles) in length. For example, the light, fine, threads of an ordinary nylon will weigh less and therefore have a lower denier than that of a beefier, ballistic-strength nylon. How will you know what kind of fabric is used in your tent? Manufacturers and retailers recognize the influence such specifications can have on the purchasing decisions of experienced campers and readily publicize this data in their promotional literature. An increasing number of mail-order catalogs and Internet retailers are doing the same.

Most soft goods you'll find on the camping market, such as tents and sleeping bags, are made of either polyester or nylon cloth. Polyester tends to hold its shape well and it resists degradation from ultraviolet light better than nylon, though it may be comparatively a little bulkier. Taffeta fabric has a silky, supple texture and is often used in sleeping bag liners. Ripstop material will have a visible grid of coarser threads woven into it to resist tearing. Oxford cloth is usually a little thicker and heavier than normal and is sometimes used in the floors of large tents where extra weight is not a concern.

The material in your tent or sleeping bag will be joined together with rows of stitching. Two parallel rows of stitching, called double stitching, will be stronger than one; some seams are even triple stitched. Lap-felled seams are the strongest possible seams as the opposing edges of material to be joined are folded around each other before being double stitched, which results in four layers of fabric being through-stitched instead of two. All good quality tents use lap-felled seams in their floors, while the best tents use them throughout.

~

Repair small tears in your tent with pine pitch, which you have softened by chewing.

~

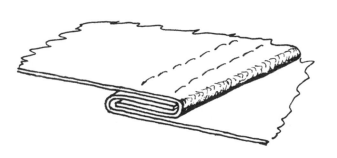

Lap-felled seams, where the edges of the fabric are folded over one another before being double-row stitched, are the strongest possible seams for tents.

Like all woven fabrics, nylon and polyester have tiny spaces between the yarns, and therefore, all are considered "breathable" unless treated with other substances, such as polyurethane. Manufacturers measure the effectiveness of any particular waterproof coating by attaching a swatch of fabric to the bottom of a long, empty, vertical tube that is slowly filled with water; at the point the fabric begins to allow water to pass through, the depth of the water in the tube is noted in millimeters, as in "The waterproof floors of the Acme Super Tent have been rated at 3,000 mm!" However, even when material has been treated to be waterproof, the needle holes of the stitching can allow water to seep through unless they are sealed with a strip of waterproof tape or treated by the consumer after he purchases the item.

If you are seeking some measure of breathability out of fabric that needs to keep water out, many products on the market today use a membrane of polytetrafluoroethylene (PTFE) bonded to nylon cloth. PTFE, the functional component of Gore-Tex, is a very thin film of Teflon that has 9 billion holes per square inch; these pores are way too small to allow liquid water to pass through, but large enough for air and water vapor. Most tents on the market that use this type of material are intended for high-altitude mountaineering and are not especially suitable for motorcycle camping.

TENTS

Tents have come a long way in the past few decades. Gone are the days when a tent was made of heavy canvas duck, used wood and steel poles as thick as a man's wrist, packed up no smaller than a side of beef and weighed almost as much. Oh, and don't forget the pungent aroma. Canvas tents, like old, sweaty gym bags, had a scent that no one could ever forget. A motorcycle camper of the past was forced to dedicate a significant portion of his bike's carrying capacity to his tent. It was, by far, the largest single item in his camping kit and demanded special attention in securing it to his motorcycle. Today's tents, by comparison, are light as a feather and pack up unbelievably small, but despite all the years of design evolution and technological improvement, the purpose of a tent has remained unchanged: to provide one with shelter from hot sun, cold winds, rain, snow, dew, insects, and other undesirables. Modern tents do all this

~

Waterproof your tent by brushing on a solution of paraffin wax and turpentine.

~

This is a top quality tent without its fly. Note multiple aluminum poles, ample ventilation, and bathtub floor. Not visible is the second entryway. Photo courtesy of The Coleman Company

and more. In fact, your biggest dilemma just might be choosing from the many, many superb tents on the market today.

One could easily argue that you don't need any special equipment to camp—and they'd find plenty of evidence to prove their case. Even today, some minimalists travel with little more than a tarp which they can string overhead or wrap around their sleeping bag for a little protection from the elements. Shops that sell high-tech mountaineering equipment may carry overbags or bivy sacks (short for "bivouac") that attempt to put a modern spin on going super light. Cut just a little larger than the average sleeping bag, these things consist of little more than a breathable shell and hood (sometimes with a zippered mesh ventilation panel) and are meant to provide emergency shelter with an absolute bare minimum of niceties. Unless this appeals to you in the very strictest sense, they are not very practical for routine camping.

TENT RATINGS

Determining which tent rating is best for you involves evaluating how and when you intend to use it. Do you only occasionally camp on a nice summer outing, or do you regularly attend early or late season rallies in the Rockies? And what about that trip you have planned across the Alcan Highway?

The overwhelming majority of tents on the market are rated for three-season use, for camping out in the spring, summer, and fall. Although the definition may sound like it limits these tents to only moderate conditions, in truth, the best tents in this category are very versatile and should be able to handle just about any conditions un-

Side view of my favorite Eureka Mountain Pass 2XT without the fly.

And with the fly. Note the added square footage both in front and back.

With the front fly door unzipped you can see half of the weather-protected front storage area. This is the vestibule. A similar area is at the rear of the tent. Footwear is always left here, never in the tent.

To be effective, flies are suspended above the tent canopy and reach within three inches of the ground ALL THE WAY AROUND.

der which the average person might find himself camping, from dry desert heat, to summer thunder squalls, to fringe season snowstorms! Three-season tents are typically constructed as double-wall systems, with the main body of the tent designed to maximize ventilation, and a separate overhead fly to actually protect you from the elements. More on this later.

At both the extreme high and low ends of the price spectrum, you will find single-wall tents, none of which are truly ideal for motorcycle camping. The most economical single wall tents are constructed of waterproof fabric with taped or sealed seams to keep weather out. As you might expect, they also tend to seal in the heat and condensation of your breath, and hence, can get unbearably dank if you are in them for any length of time without any other means for ventilation. On the other end, you will find expensive, single-wall mountaineering shelters which are often constructed from nylon bonded to a waterproof, breathable, PTFE membrane, such as Gore-Tex. Expedition tents meant for use in winter conditions are designed to withstand all manner of high-alpine or arctic weather; in keeping with their priorities, however, the features they sport can be so highly specialized as to be of little use under less extreme conditions.

TENT ANATOMY

The main body of a tent, or shell, consists of a canopy joined to a floor. The weights of the fabrics used in tent canopies can vary across

~

A fly will make the tent roof waterproof and the tent cooler during the day.

~

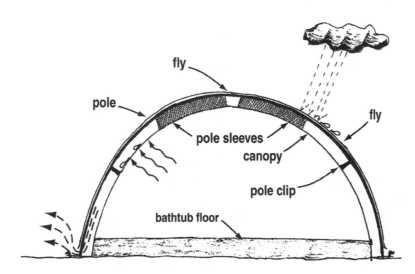

Tent flies are not just for looks. They create a vital waterproof air space over the main tent body that is a channel for the outflow of moist air from within the tent.

The bathtub floor, unlike the upper part of the tent, which must be made of breathable fabric, is waterproofed to prevent seepage from entering the tent. Note that there is also no seam along the edge that touches the ground.

brands and models. Lighter weight fabrics are less expensive and shorter-lived, and are found only in economy tents; better quality tents use fabrics starting at 1.9 oz/yd with 70 denier yarns. Some economy tent makers would have you believe that waterproof tent canopies are a good thing, when it is really just the opposite. Fabric that has been sealed to prevent moisture from coming through to the inside will also prevent it from escaping out. Moisture and heat from your breath will accumulate inside and soon everything will be damp and clammy.

Good quality tents will deliberately leave the canopy unsealed so the tent can breathe, and use a separate waterproof rain cover called a fly. A full fly will even extend outward beyond the door of your tent, creating a useful enclosed "porch," known as a vestibule, that's an ideal place for storing boots and shoes, wet gear, and other stuff you don't want inside your tent. Not only will a fly protect your expensive tent from moisture, tree offal, insect droppings, hot sun, and UV rays, it is an important part of the double-wall system mentioned earlier. When erected properly, a fly will typically sit 3 to 4 inches above the canopy, with its bottom edges extending almost to the ground. Heat and humidity from inside the tent will easily pass into this vacant space where it will be free to circulate with fresh air entering along the base of the fly. See diagram on preceding page.

Windows and vents of fine mesh will also contribute to maintaining a comfortable environment inside your tent. An effective tent design will have at least a couple of sidewall windows to encourage cross-tent ventilation, and venting at or near the canopy peak for thermal circulation. Because windows and vents are expensive components, their number, size, and location will vary according to manufacturer, model, and price. Tent doors will often have a zippered screen as well as a solid storm panel. A few modern tents even sport two doors, a simple feature that can really make sharing a tent a heck of a lot nicer.

As important as it is for a canopy to breathe, it is just as critical that the floor of your tent form an impermeable barrier between you and the ground—but this is a job easier said than done. To begin with, floors get it from both sides: wear, tear, and abuse from feet, gear bags, boots, luggage, and everything else on the inside, and dirt, rocks, roots, and water on the outside. To stand up to all this, manufacturers typically use a durable 1.9–4-ounce fabric that has been adequately waterproofed. Floor construction can be even more important than the actual materials used, however. Mid-floor seams should be double stitched (a lap-felled seam is even better) and taped. Previous generations of tents joined the sidewalls to the floor at ground level, and sooner or later, most tents leaked along these seams. Good tents today use a bathtub floor, where the edges of the floor are turned upward several inches before they join the tent walls. To really extend the life of a tent floor, experienced campers use a ground cloth beneath their tents, a sheet of heavyweight plastic or coated nylon cut a little smaller than the footprint of their shelter. Inexpensive, discount store poly-tarps that you can cut to shape work great.

~

Tent stakes can be cut from dead wood or green. If the latter, they must first be fire-hardened.

~

The length of folded tent poles usually determines the pack size of a tent with aluminum poles having a significant advantage over fiberglass. These poles are from my Eureka Mountain Pass 2XT.

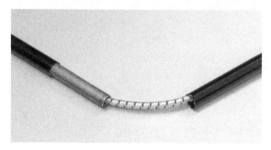

Preferred for its strength and hardness over fiberglass, aluminum pole joints with their internal fixed sleeves, have no external bits to snag on tent sleeves. Note the elastic shock cord, which runs the entire length of the pole.

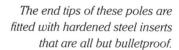

The end tips of these poles are fitted with hardened steel inserts that are all but bulletproof.

~

A canvas tent with no fly will leak in a rain at any spot even lightly touched on the inside.

~

The actual structure of any particular tent consists of shock-corded poles from which the canopy is supported or suspended via plastic clips, webbing loops, or integral sleeves of fabric. Made up of short sections of tubing which fit together, poles are usually made of resilient aluminum, though some economy brands still use fiberglass, which is heavier and more brittle. With either type, you should assemble poles gently so that you don't cause any nicks or burrs to form in the ferrules, or joints, where they connect, as that could abrade the shock cord running within. Although the aluminum industry does employ a uniform numerical system to identify different alloys, the material designations you will see in gear ads may bear little resemblance to it. Not to worry though—they're probably all fine for our purposes. The ratings do not refer to the quality of the aluminum used, but to its relative stiffness. As a buyer, you can be confident that manufacturers have chosen poles with the right amount of flexibility for the design of any particular tent.

Depending on the number of poles used and their configuration, some tents are freestanding, meaning that, theoretically at least, they will support the canopy without needing to be staked out—a bonus when you have to pitch your tent on a platform or in deep sand or bark mulch where it's hard to set a stake well. In practice, most freestanding tents will be better off staked out, especially when it's windy, and it may still be necessary to guy out your fly and vestibule if you want them to function optimally. Despite this, freestanding tents have several advantages, not the least of which is that even after they are pitched, they are easy to relocate if you should find a lump under your bed or a better view across the way. Because you can pick them up, turn them over, and even shake them out, keeping your tent dry and clean is as simple as it gets. Non-freestanding tents, however, remain very popular. They may be simpler in design (and therefore cheaper, too) and will often pack up smaller than their cousins.

TENT SIZE

When shopping for a tent, you will need to consider what size will best suit you and your needs. Some tents are only high enough to permit sitting and then only at one end of the shelter; changing clothes must be done "slither method" on one's back. Storage space may be another concern. Most manufacturers of gear aimed at backpackers are pretty stingy with interior space. As motorcyclists, however, we have a lot of bulky gear and you should expect that you would want to stow some of it inside your tent, especially if you plan to be in an area for several days and would like to ride around unencumbered by luggage. As a rule of thumb, begin by shopping for a tent that is rated for at least one more person than you plan to have in the tent, to ensure that you will not be too cramped.

Most outdoor equipment shops will let prospective customers set up tents they are considering for purchase, so you can gauge both its ease of assembly and evaluate its actual space and layout. An empty tent can look deceivingly roomy until you spread out your sleeping gear, so that makes for a good practical test. My lone air mattress occupies every bit of floor space in one maker's "two-man" tent!

Surprisingly enough, there is very little variation between the packed sizes of most three-season tents, even when their capacity is nearly double that of others in the category. It is the length of the pole sections that determines the length of a tent package, and most end up measuring between 18 and 24 inches long and 4 to 7 inches in diameter. The weight that is added when you double your tent capacity is also fairly negligible to us motorcyclists (between 1 and 3 pounds). All this speaks to the fact that there simply isn't much to be gained by choosing a very small tent, so allow yourself the luxury of a little more space and you'll be the happier for it.

~

The best type of tent is a lean-to or any tent with an open front. A fire built immediately in front will then have its heat reflected down upon the occupants.

~

For many of us, the A-frame, "pup tent" was our first introduction to tenting. Though still available it is rarely seen today.

~

Tee Pee-style tents are good because you can build a fire inside.

~

TENT DESIGNS

After you have given some thought to when and how you will be using your tent, and what features will be most important to you, it's time to look at which models will do the job. There are basically five different types of tents out there, and you are likely to see them all well-represented at a typical motorcycle rally. Some designs will have inherently more useable interior space than others, due perhaps to having more vertical sidewalls. Others might be more stable in stormy weather. Still others might be so simple and time-tested as to ring bells on the economic scale—especially if you are perfectly willing to compromise on the few features you figure you'll be missing.

A-Frame Tents

Dating back to the days of field infantry, the classic pup tent design persists in its very simplicity—three or four sticks, a bit of cord, a tarp, and you're done. Modern versions, such as the Wenzel Starlite are considerably more sophisticated, boasting heavy-duty integrated floors and walls, UV-protected fabric, mesh vents, and hefty fiberglass poles. The steeply sloping sidewalls of an A-frame tent, however, really limit the amount of useable headroom you have. These tents must be staked out and guy lines need to be taut, as an unsupported ridgeline can have a tendency to sag, especially in damp weather.

The modified A-frame tent with its external frame is still favored by many campers.

Modified A-Frame Tents

Manufacturers tried to better the original A-frame design by improving both headroom and structural stability. Campers enjoy ample room to sit, dress, and even stand in larger models. External frames and horizontal ridgepoles add considerable strength and allow the use of a rain fly, which, in turn, permits the addition of a vestibule. Motorcyclists won't find the corresponding increase in weight and packed size of much consequence. Eureka is one of the most prolific makers of A-frame tents so check out their complete line for these as well as other style tents.

Hoop Tents

Also known as tunnel tents, hoop tents are for the minimalist camper who wants to tote the smallest possible load. Just how small are they? A good example is the Clip Flashlight by Sierra Designs. When rolled up, the tent (less poles) fits in the palm of a man's hand and weighs only 1 1/2 pounds! With fly, poles, stakes, and stuff sack, it weighs in just a little over four pounds. The development of strong, flexible materials for poles led tent designers to use inverted U-shaped hoops placed fore and aft from which they suspend the canopy. A fly is secured over the top of the hoops to form a ventilation space. Like an A-frame, these tents need to be staked out and guyed well or the unsupported canopy can sag. Hoop tents are quick and easy to pitch and are great for bikers who are jammed for luggage space or anyone who simply wants to go as light as possible. I have used one for years with very satisfactory results, though I will admit that storage space is very limited and changing clothes can be a bit of a contortionist's feat.

For backpackers and space-conscious bikers, there's nothing better than the modified hoop tent. The tent on the left is my Sierra Designs Clip Flashlight 2. It rolls up (not including poles) into a package that fits in the palm of my hand and weighs only 3lbs, 6oz complete.

The most popular tent design today is the dome tent. They're available in a huge variety of sizes and colors. Quality also varies greatly, from very, very bad to excellent. Shown here, without flies, are my Mountain Pass 2XT, (L) and Aurora 4 (R), both three-season tents by Eureka. In the middle is a four-season Coleman Exponent Lynx 3. All are outstanding tents.

Dome Tents

Dome tents have been a hit with campers ever since materials like lightweight nylon and flexible aluminum first made them practical. The basic geodesic designs create symmetrical or nearly symmetrical free-standing structures with little unsupported fabric. Today you will see dome tents sold in every size, rating, price, and color you can imagine—truly something for everyone. They are easy to set up and their igloo shape can yield a lot of useable interior space.

Cabin Tents

With four nearly vertical walls, a peaked roof, and room for numerous people, you can see where cabin tents got their name. Cabin tents today, however, are a mixed lot. While many still use the same traditional architecture, others have begun to resemble large dome tents. Of course, stellar attributes, such as headroom to spare, multiple rooms, and floor space enough for a dance party have their price. These tents are heavy, take up a lot of room, and tend to have very long poles, making them an impractical choice for motorcycle camping unless you use a cargo trailer.

Cabin tents are the roomiest of all; unfortunately they can be very heavy and bulky. Still, they're a viable option for cargo trailers.

Since the first edition of this book, tent manufacturers, in an attempt to scale back costs, have also scaled back on the quality of many of their products. Lighter fabrics instead of heavier and tougher, fiberglass poles instead of aluminum, and partial flies rather than full length are just a few of the cost-cutting measures. When shopping for a good quality tent remember first that while bargain basement priced tents from big-box discount stores are proof of the mantra that you get what you pay for, you can't always be sure that fancy brand name and high price will always be a guarantee of a good product either. Be a wise shopper and make your choice based on what you've learned here.

SLEEPING BAGS

Sleeping well is very, very important—especially to us motorcyclists who place a high priority on being alert in the saddle each day. A good sleeping bag and ground pad can go a long way toward ensuring that you will get a good night's rest. And, in turn, your overall camping experience will just be that much more enjoyable. Many people start camping with the ubiquitous rectangular bags aimed at family campers. They are, after all, inexpensive and roomy, even if they are bulky. But as you camp more and more, you may begin to notice the ways in which they fall well short from being an ideal bed. If you are planning to upgrade your gear, start by shopping for a better sleeping bag, as that improvement is likely to make the biggest difference to you.

In a way, sleeping bags are actually less pieces of gear then they are clothing for nightwear. Clothing helps us to regulate body temperature and comes in a virtually endless variety of styles, shapes, and sizes to suit myriad types of people and conditions. Think of sleeping bags like that. As we sleep, our nighttime metabolism drops, and we need more insulation to maintain body comfort than we would otherwise in our active, waking state. The fill in your sleeping bag traps air to both insulate you from the cold outside and conserve the heat generated by your own body. Old-fashioned rectangular bags simply cannot do this very efficiently. Semi-rectangular bags have a modestly tapered cut that narrows toward the foot, decreasing the amount of air space one has to keep warm without their being too claustrophobic.

~

There are fat trees and thin trees. The former will be struck by lightning more often than the latter. Examples of fat trees are maple, oak, butternut, and birch. Examples of thin trees are catalpas, locusts, and willow.

~

Sleeping bags come in different sizes. Bags that are sized for children are not gimmicks; smaller bags greatly increase warmth for small bodies on cold nights.

~

Stacked firewood will stay dryer in rain and make your camp look neater.

~

Once you step away from the bargain bin, most modern sleeping bags are mummy-shaped, which conforms well to the general contours of an average human while eliminating the unnecessary fabric and extra insulation found in a rectangular bag. There are many variations on the basic mummy theme, and each manufacturer prides himself on having the best design of all. Of course, it will be for you to decide. Some models are available in regular as well as long sizes for extra-tall campers. Scaled-down versions of adult bags are even available for children, an important consideration if you often bring your kids along. Youngsters can have a terrible time sleeping comfortably in adult bags, as there's just too much vacant space for their smaller bodies to heat. Since camping trips should provide young people with the sort of adventures they will remember all their lives, you want to make sure that their memories are positive ones.

A reputable gear outfitter will encourage you to "try on" a sleeping bag, just as you would a new suit, to see if it fits you properly. After removing your shoes and crawling inside, take a moment to notice how well the zippers function, both from the inside as well as the outside. The interior of the bag should be in loose contact with your body, and it should not constrict you across the shoulders or hips. A properly fitting bag is not like a bed at home in which the occupant has freedom of movement within. Rather, a sleeping bag should gently hug one's body, moving and turning with it, so as to permit complete freedom of movement while eliminating heat-robbing air gaps.

FEATURES AND BENEFITS

There are so many details that go into constructing a good sleeping bag that you may not truly appreciate them—until you need them. First off, during sleep the average human gives off a surprising amount of moisture in the form of both perspiration and respiration. Just as tents should be designed to breathe, the shell of a good sleeping bag needs to allow humidity to escape before it can dampen the loft of your insulation. The cotton and flannel linings of low-end bags may feel nice initially, but they are especially bad when it comes to retaining moisture that will conduct heat away from your body.

In fact, almost all of the features one must look for in a good sleeping bag are designed to increase the efficiency of your sleeping system should the weather turn unexpectedly cold. Did I hear you say you're not going to camp when it's cold? Don't bet on it. During Daytona Bike Week, nighttime temperatures can (and frequently do) drop into the 30s and 40s. I have been caught in unseasonable snows in the mountains out west and have had my share of bone-cold rain. And it doesn't have to be really cold out either; under the wrong conditions, you can be miserable when temps are in the 50s and 60s. At

Look beyond the fancy colors and name on a sleeping bag to its construction details. Zipper guards to prevent snagging and draft tubes to keep out cold air are just two features to look for.

Compare the packed size of two sleeping bags, both with the same temperature rating. The smaller bag above contains micro-fiber insulation, while the bag below contains Hollofil II. This difference is critical for space concious hikers and bikers.

times like these it's critical to be able to retain every bit of body heat within your sleeping bag.

A hood that you can draw snugly around your head can really make a big difference when it comes to staying warm. Really good sleeping bags may also have a separate draft collar around your neck to ensure that warm air around the core of your body cannot escape easily. Another chink in your defenses exists along the length of your zipper; an insulating draft tube that hangs down to overlap the leak can make a huge difference. Speaking of zippers, they only work if they work. Fortunately, most reputable gear manufacturers usually don't skimp too much on the actual zippers of their sleeping bags; it's too important. However, a zipper that snags easily on all that surrounding material can be just as bad. Some makers have taken to sewing stiff, narrow strips of fabric tape along the entire length of the zipper to shield it, or the fabric adjacent to the zipper itself may be stiffened with several rows of stitches.

INSULATION

When selecting a sleeping bag, one of the first things you'll have to decide is how much warmth you'll need. Bag makers try to help you out with this aspect by rating their bags for different temperatures. Sometimes they'll list one number, say 40° F, which means the bag should be useful if the outside temperature drops to that point. Other times they'll list a range, 15/30° F, for example. Ratings are not to be taken as gospel, however, but as starting points in the process of selecting a sleeping bag. Remember, the primary heat source—the oc-

~

The ideal camp bed is two pair of blankets with a waterproof undersheet, all on top of a bed of pine boughs.

~

The same two bags again, lying open. The thicker bag in the rear contains Hollofil II; the bag in front contains Thermolite Micro.

cupant's own body—will vary widely between individuals, just as you will see some folks happily wearing T-shirts while others shiver in sweatshirts. Sleeping bag makers refer to those at opposite ends of the extreme as cold sleepers and hot sleepers. Campers on either end of the spectrum should adjust the bag ratings by 10 to 15 degrees F. If you are in doubt, choose a bag that you're sure will keep you warm. It's easier to cool off a hot bag than make a cold one warmer.

The type of insulation used in your sleeping bag is another important but easily confusing choice, as there are so many different types and brand names available. The important thing for space conscious motorcycle campers to know is that some materials are inherently more efficient than others, so they can do the same amount of work with less bulk and weight.

An insulation's capacity to function well is dependent on how well it can fluff up and trap air. Good sleeping bags will have a differentially cut liner that is actually smaller than the outer shell, to ensure that there is plenty of room for the insulation to loft. Economy bags may be quilt-stitched through the shell, fill, and lining in one go, which results in the insulation being compressed until it has virtually no insulating powers. In better designs, the insulation is trapped in three-dimensional channels called baffles, which may be shaped so as to be staggered shingle-style over one another to all but eliminate cold spots. A good foot box which allows the insulation to loft fully while eliminating heat-stealing leaks also will show evidence of a great deal of thought on the part of the designer.

Down Insulation

Before the development of synthetic materials, sleeping bags insulated with goose down were considered the finest that money could buy. Many campers still agree. When comparing sleeping bags of the

~

To make a spoon, lash a half oyster shell into the end of a split stick.

~

ALL-PURPOSE REPAIR KIT CONTENTS

A fact of camping life is that, sooner or later, something is going to break. It happens to everyone whether they're "camping" in a half-million-dollar motor home, or a hundred-dollar dome tent. The secret is knowing how to fix what's broken and having the tools and parts on hand to do the job. Fortunately, most of the repairs needed for motorcycle camping equipment require only a relatively small assortment of tools and odd bits of stuff. Everything can be easily carried in a small pouch.

There may be other tools required such as pliers, but those are already in the bike tool kit.

- ☐ Sewing kit with needles, thread, buttons, and safety pins
- ☐ Dental floss (for heavy-duty sewing)
- ☐ Ripstop nylon repair tape
- ☐ Alcohol swabs (for cleaning surfaces to be repaired)
- ☐ Urethane adhesive and/or sleeping pad repair kit
- ☐ Duct tape (several yards wound around a pen, flashlight, or wooden dowel rod)
- ☐ Extra nylon cord
- ☐ 3-inch piece of aluminum tubing (for splinting cracked tent poles)
- ☐ Tube of Gel Super Glue
- ☐ Stove repair kit, with spare parts
- ☐ Safety pins of various sizes ■

same general quality and temperature rating, a down bag almost always will be lighter and more packable than a comparable sleeping bag that uses synthetic insulation—although the gap has admittedly narrowed over the years as scientists learn to mimic the best qualities of down insulation with high-tech fibers. Down bags also resume their fully lofted shape quicker after being unpacked than do synthetic bags. Loft characteristics are typically compared by measuring the number of cubic centimeters occupied by one ounce of fill. Most good three-season down bags use down rated in the 600–650cc range; winter weight bags will use 750–800cc fill down and may attain temperature ratings good to –40 F!

Although down bags are criticized for being expensive, they are usually pretty comparable in price to synthetic bags of similar ratings, features, and quality. The most significant disadvantage of down is that it will lose just about all of its ability to loft (and therefore insulate) if it gets wet. And, if it does get soaked, it can be a real hassle to dry out. At the very least, down bags should be aired out thoroughly whenever possible and campers who use down sleeping bags should be committed to keeping them dry. Without a good system of baffles, down also can be prone to shifting around and leaving cold spots. If you are inspecting a sleeping bag, ensure that the shell fabric is woven tightly enough to prevent feathers from working their way out.

Synthetic Insulation – What's New
The technology of synthetic insulations has progressed dramatically since their introduction several decades ago. At first they consisted merely of synthetic fibers stuffed between a sleeping bag's inner and outer liners, but it was soon discovered that they just didn't entrap enough dead air to insulate very efficiently. Scientists solved this problem by making the fibers hollow, first with one long hole through them like a water pipe, then with multiple holes for even better heat retention characteristics. The newest developments, however, seemingly bring the technology full circle. Microfiber insulations, the lightest, most compact, and most efficient of all synthetic insulations, once again use solid fibers, but they are ultra-small in diameter.

There are many different brands of sleeping bags with synthetic insulation available, with a variety of names given to the insulation in the bags. While there used to be only a few different types of insulating materials made by just two or three companies, now instead of listing the actual trade names of the insulation material, it seems that the bag makers' marketing departments have made up new names to distinguish their bags from those of their competitors.

This much has not changed—the type of insulating material used in a bag is exceedingly important as it is the single most critical factor in affecting a bag's ability to perform, that is, keeping its occupant dry and warm. Microfiber insulations are still by far the best of the

~

Recipe for good, fast coffee: boil water then insert a tied muslin bag containing ground coffee. After five minutes it's ready to drink.

~

101

synthetic insulations not only because they perform better than the older hollow core fibers, but because of their volume. Bags using microfibers are very much smaller than bags using other materials, a very important asset for space-conscious motorcycle campers. The challenge for the buyer has become discerning which bags are microfiber-equipped and which ones aren't.

The most obvious way to find a microfiber bag is to check the hang tag. Though the name of the insulation material may be something else, the written description could contain the term microfiber. If it doesn't, then remember that size matters. Microfiber bags can often be identified as bags that are noticeably smaller than other bags containing older materials rated for the same temperature range. Where older technology bags are typically 12 to 14 inches in diameter when rolled up, microfiber bags may only be 6 to 8 inches.

Another clue that microfiber insulations are used is that the bags will usually be more expensive than those containing cheaper materials. Be aware though, this last clue is normally true when comparing bags of the same brand name but less so between brands as some makers put high prices even on older technology bags.

In the event that bags can be found which still use the original names of the insulating materials the following descriptions will still be of use.

Hollofil 808 is one of the granddaddies of synthetic insulation. A single-hole insulation, 808 is made from pre-consumer recycled polyester. It continues to be used in clothing and inexpensive sleeping bags.

Hollofil II is a four-hole insulation, so it traps more air and offers more warmth than the 808. It's still used in less expensive bags and is well suited for warm weather camping.

Quallofil is the latest and best performing of the multi-hole polyester fibers. Each strand of Quallofil has seven longitudinal air channels for entrapping the maximum amount of air. It's found in moderately priced to expensive bags.

Thermolite Micro is the lightest of Dupont's new solid-core microfibers. It offers a third more warmth per inch of loft than down, while being very compact and non-allergenic. This is a great insulation for three-season use.

Thermolite Extreme is Dupont's most high-tech microfiber and the best insulator yet developed. This solid core insulation is actually a

~

To dry out wet or damp boots, drop in a few handfuls of pebbles which you have heated in a frying pan. By morning they should be dry.

~

blend of microfibers, slightly larger bonding fibers, and hollow-core spring fibers. Typically found in bags rated from 0 F to –40 F.

Polarguard HV is a continuous filament, solid core, polyester microfiber. It offers good compressibility and minimal weight for high-end bags intended for use in moderately cold conditions.

Polarguard 3D is many experts' choice for optimum performance in very cold conditions. Like Polarguard HV, this product is also a continuous filament microfiber, 100 percent polyester. Both have a unique triangular cross-section which prevents the fibers from collapsing. Polarguard 3D has been chosen by the U.S. Armed services for use in their "Extreme Cold Weather Sleep System" bags. Found commercially in high-end bags that may be rated to as low as –60 F.

Finally, buyers may also find value in consulting websites devoted to reviewing outdoor gear (found by entering "outdoor gear review" into an Internet search engine). There are many of these on the Internet, so many that sites may be found originating in almost any country and in any language. Due to the fast changing nature of the Internet it is impractical to identify particular sites. But as of this writing the site www.trailspace.com contained well-written reviews of all types of camping gear.

PADS, MATTRESSES, AND COTS

Steadfast non-campers are constantly railing against sleeping on the ground. Well guess what . . . most campers don't. Sleeping on the ground is cold and uncomfortable, no matter how good a sleeping bag is. And, unless the piece of earth chosen for a campsite is in a cli-

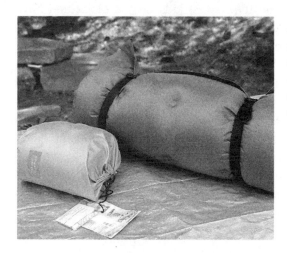

Self-inflating thermal sleeping pads are popular with a great many campers though they consume a lot of space. In front is a hi-tech Exped 7.5 air mattress from Switzerland that fully inflates in less than two minutes without blowing in.

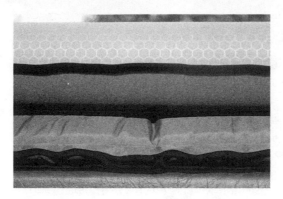

Thickness comparison: the Exped air mattress is on top of the thermal pad.

~

Tents intended to be used in cold weather should not have floors.

~

mate that stays very warm at night, heat from a warm human body will dissipate quickly into the cooler earth.

Since the days of the earliest native peoples and continuing well up into the 1900s, this problem was resolved by making beds of boughs upon which to lay blankets. Elaborate, and by today's standards, charming descriptions and endorsements for this technique are to be found in the classic camping works of early woodcraft writers.

Fortunately there are better alternatives to choose from today: foam pads, mattress pads, and air mattresses.

Closed-cell foam pads, as the name implies, are made up of tiny, hollow plastic bubbles or cells. These pads have the advantage of being lightweight, very inexpensive, and just about foolproof. Open-cell foam pads are similar to a kitchen sponge and will soak up water just as easily. Many campers find them comfortable but they are extremely bulky and really not suitable for motorcycle camping.

Self-inflating pads are the newest kids on the block and have gained an amazing following, outselling the other types of mattresses by a wide margin. They use a sheet of open-cell foam that is encased in a waterproof, airtight envelope of nylon. To pack up, the valve at one corner of the mat is opened to allow excess air to be squeezed out as the mat is rolled up tightly, after which the valve is closed to prevent the air from reentering. Upon unpacking, the valve is opened allowing the open-cell foam to slowly return to its uncompressed shape. You can then close the air valve. Depending on your own personal tough-guy quotient you can choose pads varying from 1 1/2 to 3 inches thick in full-length (72–76 inches) or three-quarter versions (approximately 48 inches). Standard width is 20 inches but wider 25-

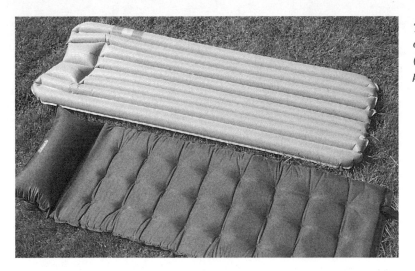

inch versions are available for larger customers. The chief advantage of self-inflating pads is their overall comfort and ease of use. On the down side, they aren't cheap, especially when compared to low-tech alternatives like closed-cell foam pads. Over time you may also find that the internal foam loses some of its shape memory, and you will have to add a few puffs of air to reach your desired level of firmness. Campers who use a self-inflating mattress should also take care not to puncture it, though fixing it in the field isn't too difficult if you are prepared with a repair kit.

Ordinary air mattresses really take a bad rap from campers who have been seduced by all the high-tech sales speak surrounding self-inflating pads. Air mattresses are roundly criticized for being heavy, difficult to inflate, and easily punctured. But the reality is that their weights are reasonable and as far as susceptibility to puncturing, they are no more so than self-inflating pads. Bear in mind these are not the less-than-ten-buck-backyard-pool versions for kids. The mats specifically engineered for campers and backpackers are well-constructed units of rubberized cotton or heavy-duty vinyl. Some come complete with built-in pillows. And at 3 to 4 inches thick, they give side sleepers more comfort than thinner self-inflating pads.

TIP: as all types of mattresses rely on air retention, campers are wise to carry a puncture repair kit, just in case.

Traditional camp cots have never been very popular with motorcycle campers, made as they were of bulky materials like lumber, steel, and heavy canvas duck. Even if they weren't so cumbersome,

~

To make a dinner knife, lash a flattened piece of tin into the end of a split stick.

~

they usually sagged down in the middle until you were bumping up against the supporting wooden crossbars. And, old-fashioned cots were originally meant to be used in old-fashioned cabin tents, whose shape and size lent themselves to furniture of typical designs and proportions. That type of cot simply wouldn't fit in most modern tents. Today, a couple of manufacturers are wedding current materials with thoughtful designs to produce cots that are a lot more manageable. The Go-Kot, available from Whitehorse Gear, packs down to 5 × 28 inches and weighs only 8 pounds. Once assembled, the 75 × 26 inch bed doesn't sag and since it sits nice and low, it will fit in all but the very smallest of tents. Cots are popular with those who have the luxury of added space afforded by cargo trailers.

LIGHTING

Experienced campers know that when it comes to light at night, three types of light sources are required. The first is a lamp that is able to stand upright by itself and throw a lot of light over a wide area. When it comes to setting up a tent at night, illuminating the inside of a tent, or lighting up a picnic table, this type of light is invaluable. Anyone who has ever camped with a Coleman lantern is not likely to forget the brilliant white light and the unique hissing sound of fuel burning inside the glass globe. Invented in 1900 as a replacement for coal oil lamps, young W.C. Coleman's lamp was quickly adopted for

A powerful yet collapsible electric lantern works great in and out of the tent.

Complementing the larger lantern are a candle lantern, single diode flashlight, and double diode headlamp. I find all four lights to be required equipment.

use in areas of the country that had neither natural gas lighting nor electricity. Since the lamp was easily portable it soon also became a favorite in the new pastime of camping—a position it still holds. Unfortunately for motorcycle campers, the relatively large size of these table lanterns, the fragility of the glass globe and silk mantels, and the problems of carrying and replenishing their special liquid fuel make them unsuitable for motorcycle camping. In their stead are a whole host of battery-powered fluorescent lanterns and the newest LED versions, some of which mimic the look of a traditional lantern. A current favorite of ours is a Coleman single-tube design, which telescopes open and shut, making it nice and compact for traveling.

In addition to a table lantern, a hand-held flashlight is necessary. Nothing fancy here, a simple and ordinary light using no more than two AA batteries is sufficient. These are for finding your way around at night or for looking through a ditty bag in the tent for that elusive candy bar without waking everybody else. Stow this light at night in exactly the same spot and where it is within reach. It will quickly become second nature to find it in the dark when needed.

Headlamps are the third type of light required. Since the first edition of this book, headlamps using LEDs (light emitting diodes) have become inexpensive and all but totally replaced earlier versions using "old fashioned" incandescent bulbs. And besides giving off more and whiter light, LEDs virtually never burn out and use much less power, meaning that batteries last several times longer. Headlamps are invaluable when tasks require the use of both hands such as bike repairing or lighting a campfire.

CORD

At the beginning of each camping season, buy a hank of cotton clothesline at the hardware store. By the time the camping season is over, the rope will be too. Where does it go? It will be used for clotheslines (for drying shower towels), for hanging food bags in trees, for guying tarps, replacing torn tent stake loops, and as gifts to neighboring campers who need a piece of rope. Many of the lesser expensive synthetic ropes are not recommended, as they're the very devil to knot and cut ends fray uncontrollably. A better value are the slightly more expensive nylon or braided cords as they are normally exempt from these problems. If there is any doubt, try tying a couple of knots. Passing the cut ends through the flame of a match melts the nylon enough to fuse the strands to prevent raveling. The ends can be shaped before the nylon cools completely.

KNIVES

There are two kinds of campers: those who carry knives, and those who borrow them from others. Knives are useful for a wide range of chores including opening packages, removing insulation from wire, slicing food, filleting fish, cutting rope, preparing kindling wood, removing splinters, and eating sardines. Knives share a long tradition with camping. As the necessity for long, fixed-bladed knives has diminished, camp knives have evolved into smaller versions with folding blades that can be carried in a small belt sheath or tucked away in a pocket. Many campers get along fine with a two-bladed lock-back pocketknife, such as those made by the famous W.R. Case and Sons in Bradford, New York. Others prefer the Swiss Army-type knife, with their proliferation of built-in accessory tools, like can openers, pliers, tweezers, and screwdrivers. A more recent variation, which has surged in popularity of late, are the somewhat larger multi-tool knives, such as those made by Leatherman. Whichever style you decide on, expect to pay a modest amount for high-quality materials and workmanship that won't let you down.

Warning: Millions of pocketknives and multitool knives are imported from the Far East each year, most of which are of very poor quality. A camper's knife is very important. Blades and tools that break, dull, and rust quickly due to poor steel cannot be tolerated.

~

An acetylene lantern is a good source of light. A carbide lantern is excellent, also, and better than kerosene. Even one drop of kerosene can taint all your food with an obnoxious odor.

~

Knives, too, come in a variety of shapes and sizes. Left to right: Case pocketknife, Swiss style army knife by Wenger, camp and hunting knives by the author, and multi-tool knife by Carolina Knife and Tool.

The Case Sodbuster belt knife is a very utilitarian knife that has innumerable uses around a camp. The belt carrying case means the knife is easy to get to when needed.

The three knives that I always take camping are the Stag handle Canoe pocketknife, Sodbuster belt knife, and Red Stag Hunter, all by WR Case & Sons.

With its hard plastic handles and 3 $^5/_8$ inch stainless steel blade the Sodbuster belt knife is impervious to the nastiest of weather.

Sitting on a chair instead of the ground will make you feel positively civilized. The two options that are most popular with motorcycle campers are the custom-made, hardwood frame Kermit Chair and the ever-available discount store special.

CAMP CHAIRS

There is nothing that compares to a simple chair for making a camper feel comfortable after a long day riding, hiking, or just walking around visiting. Just try getting by without one to see why. But hauling chairs around the country on the back of a bike can present a problem. They're frequently heavy and take up a lot of space. In fact, the majority of chairs used by campers are more suited for large RVs than motorcycles. Most are made of heavy canvas with large aluminum frames that, when folded up and stowed in their carrying bags, measure about five inches in diameter by 35 inches in length. Now that's a lot of volume for a biker not to mention it's a very ungainly hunk to contend with, but there are alternatives.

At the top of the list is the ever popular and super comfortable Kermit Chair, hand made by Tom Sherrill, a 43-year motorcyclist in Nashville, Tenn. Constructed of hardwood, 1,000 denier nylon, aluminum and stainless steel, the chair has been around since 1984 and

Both chairs packed up for traveling. The Kermit chair is on the bottom.

Another option is the three-legged stool for the obsessive space-savers.

has been successfully road tested by over 10,000 bike campers. Additionally, the chair carries a five-year warranty and has been tested at 750 lbs. It weighs 4 pounds and packs to 4 by 22 inches.

Other light-weight options include a foldable, stadium style seat back. These are commonly seen advertised in outdoor gear catalogs. The bottom of this seat actually sits on the ground and a vertical back is hinged to the bottom and supported by two fabric straps. Its advantages are its ultra light weight (1 1/2 lbs) and low volume. It folds in half to about 15 inches square by 1 inch thick. The disadvantage is that one's butt is on the ground whether it's dry, cold, or wet. I don't recommend it and have rarely, if ever, seen it in use.

Stools are a third option, but with pack sizes near to or as large as that of the Kermit Chair why bother?

TIP: Regardless of the type of chair you opt for put your name on it as chairs tend to get mixed up quite easily when camping with others.

But does it really save space? Folded for traveling the stool is the same size as the wonderfully comfortable Kermit chair.

A great invention is this lightweight collapsible table that's just the ticket for those times when a picnic table isn't available. The inset shows how compact the table is when it is collapsed.

COOKING GEAR

Camp cooking is more thoroughly taken up in Chapter 11. The following is a review of the gear required.

STOVES

Camp cooking requires a surprisingly small amount of gear: a stove, a pot and pan, utensils, and a few miscellaneous items. These days, it seems like there are hundreds of camp stoves on the market that could probably do your bidding when it comes to making pasta and hot chocolate. If your cooking style is a little more sophisticated, you might find other features valuable as well, such as the ability to modulate a blowtorch-like flame for a nice simmer.

Campers typically use stoves that burn either liquid fuel or pressurized gas. The fuel supply for either type may be mounted directly below the pot platform or connected via a hose to a tank that sits beside the stove. Both are excellent, but the latter type may sit lower and, hence, be more inherently stable; these stoves also break down into smaller components for packing up. If you plan to use especially large pots and pans, make sure they will not spread the flame from your burner dangerously close to your remote fuel supply.

You can do a lot to stretch the life of your fuel supply, of whatever type, by practicing a few good habits: don't light your stove until you're ready to start cooking; don't run it hotter than necessary; cover a pot or pan to markedly reduce the amount of time needed to heat the contents; shut the fuel off as soon as possible; and use the windscreen that is supplied with your stove or form one out of aluminum foil.

Liquid-Fuel Stoves

Liquid-fuel stoves date back to the venerable old two-burner camp stoves with their attached fuel reservoirs that one filled with clean-burning Coleman fuel, known generically as white gas. As the backpacking craze of the 1970s gained momentum, liquid-fuel stoves evolved into lightweight, reliable single-burner units, and some basic designs have changed little since then.

Since liquid fuel must be converted to a vapor before it will burn, these types of stoves must be primed before you light 'em up—a fairly simple routine—but one which can take a little practice at first. The reservoir tank is pressurized via a pump and a small amount of fuel is bled out into the priming cup at the base of the burner—just enough to soak the wick. Shut off the valve just as you hear the telltale hiss; remember, there will be a delay before fuel stops flowing as the remainder in the line empties into the priming cup. Once ignited, this flame will heat an exposed section of the fuel line, turning the liquid gas within to vapor. Just as this initial flame is sputtering out, you can open the valve to the pressurized fuel line and you will be in business.

There are several reasons why liquid-fuel stoves are still popular, not the least of which is that they are very economical to operate. White gas is stable, cheap, and readily available across the land,

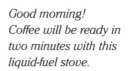

A quickly-made camp candle holder is an empty can filled with sand or soil. Insert the base of the candle an inch or two.

Good morning! Coffee will be ready in two minutes with this liquid-fuel stove.

though often it's only offered in one-gallon containers, which is usually more than you need to haul around on a typical motorcycle trip. Some newer multi-fuel stoves have been engineered to burn all manner of heavier fuels including kerosene, diesel, and unleaded gasoline (lower octanes are best). If you are planning to travel away from civilization, this could come in handy. In addition, you can restock your fuel supply a cup at a time at the pump.

The one disadvantage of liquid-fuel stoves is the extra care needed to prevent fuel spillage while en route. Spilled fuel inside a luggage compartment will leave everything reeking and flammable as well. This can easily be prevented by making sure all caps are tightly secured, storing the containers in chemical-proof bags with airtight seals and transporting those in their own luggage such as a pannier.

Pressurized Canister Gas Stoves

The other type of stove commonly carried by motorcyclists is fueled via pressurized canisters of propane, butane, isobutane, or a blend of fuels, any of which would probably function fine under the relatively temperate, low-altitude conditions under which motorcyclists usually camp. Unlike liquid-fuel stoves, they require no priming and may even have a push-button ignition similar to the one on your large gas grill at home. They're absolutely leakproof, spillproof, and odor proof, and a breeze to use.

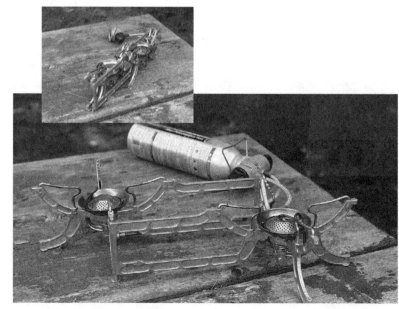

Butane gas double burner stove. Do you want bacon with your eggs? The inset shows the butane stove collapsed for transport.

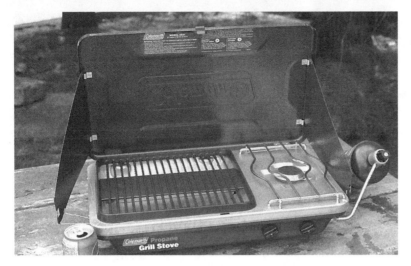

The famous old standby, now using modern propane gas, is too big for a bike, but perfect for a cargo trailer.

Their main disadvantage is that because the canisters are made of metal, it's impossible to see how much fuel is left inside, so there's a chance you could run out unexpectedly. Additionally, you could have trouble locating replacements, other than the propane variety. The alternative is to always carry spares that are compatible with your stove. All of which makes liquid multi-fuel stoves the more appealing. If you can buy gas for your bike, you've got fuel for your stove!

Because motorcycle trailer outfits are the least limited by their carrying capacity, they may be able to make use of larger gear including the legendary but still popular double burner Coleman stove.

Baking Ovens

For many self-reliant campers the ability to bake at camp is the ultimate measure of success. Suffice it to say, though, that it's always been tough to do that without at least a heavy cast-iron Dutch oven, and unless there's a cargo trailer involved in your camp, there isn't likely going to be one of those. Coming to the rescue is a clever gadget called the Outback Oven. The standard oven is comprised of a 10-inch round baking pan with lid and built in thermometer and a uniquely designed flexible heat retention cover. This assembly in turn rests atop a heat diffuser disk and riser that sits on your own cook stove. Just about anything that can be baked in a conventional oven can be baked in this. Users are warned, however, not to use the oven in combination with stoves that piggyback atop fuel reservoirs, whether liquid fuel or gas. Due to the larger than typical diameter of

~

Recommended tools to take camping: several pounds of nails of various sizes, hammer, wood saw, brace and bits, folding draw knife, hand ax, cord, wire, pliers and several yards of canvas.

~

*The four parts
of the oven:*
1. *heat reflector
   collar,*
2. *burner spacer,*
3. *hood and*
4. *thermometer.*

*Who would believe it,
an oven in a package
the size of a coffee
saucer.*

*You put the food
to be baked in the
covered pot.*

*. . . and it's ready
to bake.*

the included baking pan, the consequent increase in under-pan heat may overheat fuel canisters to an unsafe point. Freestanding stoves connected to separate fuel sources via hoses are recommended.

Alternatively, Outback also offers a smaller oven, the Ultralight-8 inch that works with the smaller size pans and lids typically found in camping sets. While not being able to bake as much at one time as its big brother, it does offer capacity sufficient for the needs of a solo camper and while also allowing the use of piggyback fuel sources. This unit weighs only 300 grams—about two thirds of a pound—and is a favorite of backpackers.

THE WOODGAS CAMPSTOVE

Without much fanfare a new camp stove has been introduced by a small company in Midwest USA. The Woodgas Campstove, by Spenton LLC, is a novel development of an old concept—using an open cylinder as both a fireplace and a cook top. Previous, so-called cylinder stoves were never very successful being clumsy, very tipsy, difficult to fuel, and even more difficult to maintain much less control burning. Now, thanks to a scientist in Colorado and an engineer in Minnesota all those problems have been overcome resulting in a product that is efficient and easy to use.

I recently tried out the mid-size XL model and found the construction of the stove to be superb. The material is high-quality stainless steel and the fit and finish are elegant (made in the USA, by the way). Even the fasteners are aluminum giving the stove a modern appearance and making it impervious to outdoor weather conditions. I noticed the double-layer stove walls and the rows of tiny holes around the top and bottom inside the burning chamber. It turns out that these are the secret to the stove's success.

The Woodgas Campstove is, in truth, a miniature forced-air convection oven. Air is forced, via a small battery-pack-operated internal fan, into the burning chamber where small bits of burnable material (twigs, pine needles, wood chips) are burned to produce woodgas, which then flows to the top of the cylinder where it is combusted producing an amazing amount of heat. You have to see it in operation to believe it. Anything combustible that is put into the burning chamber is utterly

It may not be a better mousetrap but it sure is a clever stove. The Woodgas Campstove is fueled with found materials, such as leaves, pine needles, twigs—anything that will burn, no purchased fuel required. I like it.

consumed leaving only the smallest amount of ash in the very bottom.

That highlights another feature—the stove can be fueled with just about anything combustible, as long as it fits in a burning chamber only about 4 1/2 inches in diameter. I filled (the correct term is charged) the chamber with pine needles, small twigs, and leaves to start. To my surprise the stove blasted out heat for a full thirty minutes, more than enough time to boil water and heat a meal.

If longer cooking is required, the chamber can be re-charged at any time. No messy fuel to contend with, no gas canisters to lug around. The only down side is that due to its size, 6 by 9 inches, the stove may be impractical for backpackers and many bikers. It is ideal for those towing trailers. To learn more and to obtain a list of retailers contact the company's website www.spenton.com. ■

Two nice cook sets: the stainless steel Coleman Exponent Outfitter packs away into the largest of the pans, as does the aluminum MSR Base Two-Pot Set which is ideal for baking.

~

Empty tin cans work as substitute coffee cups.

~

POTS AND PANS AND UTENSILS

Dating from the days of the venerable army G.I. mess kit, campers today have a variety of so-called nesting cook sets to choose from. As you might guess, the term nesting refers to each pan's ability to fit inside the next, thus offering a handy variety of sizes and a compact package for travel. The similarity between sets ends there, however, as a few different prices, materials, weights, and surface finishes are available. Basic cook sets as found in the discount stores and many of the larger sporting goods dealers are appealing due to their low cost, but that low cost, to no one's surprise, is a tip off that the materials may be inferior. On the other hand, sets found in outfitter's shops and catalogs may be a lot more money. What's the difference?

Assuming that you're not paying a premium for the brand name, an important factor affecting cost and quality of cookware is material weight. As any cook worth his salt (no pun intended) knows, the heavier the material the better the cookware. At one end of the weight range is the ultra-light, thin aluminum stuff and at the other are the really heavy cast-iron components. The thin aluminum pans dissipate heat poorly, cook unevenly, scorch easily, are prone to warping, and last the shortest length of time. Cast-iron dissipates heat very efficiently and evenly, will never warp, and lasts forever.

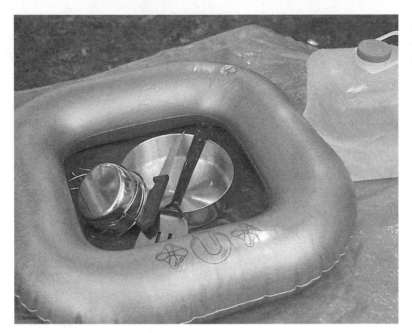

I'll wash if you dry? Sink and jug ready for KP duty.

Neither one is recommended for motorcycle campers. The former due to its poor performance and the latter due to its excessive weight and volume, in fact, cook sets of cast-iron aren't even available. Nonetheless, there are a lot of material options in between. Essentially, they range from aluminum sets of ever-increasing weights up to heavier stainless steel sets. Unlike backpackers, who must be conscious of every ounce they carry with them, motorcyclists have the luxury of opting for pots and pans of heavier material.

A non-stick coating can be a real bonus for preventing scorching and aiding in clean up. Rounded edges along the bottoms of your pots will also help to distribute heat more evenly, as will a black finish on your cookware. A small one-liter pot can hold enough water for a couple of cups of hot chocolate or a freeze-dried dinner for one; a 1.5-liter pot is usually big enough to cook a double ration of pasta. Pot lids often double as frying pans. If you like to bake in camp, non-stick cookware with tight-fitting lids are essential. For predictable baking and frying, use a heat diffuser that spreads out the flame underneath your pan.

If the nesting types of pots and pans have handles at all, they will usually fold out of the way, both to make them more packable, and to keep them from interfering with your windscreen in use; some

~

Remember that plates, buckets and cups can be made from tree bark.

~

models forego handles all together in favor of a separate pot grabber, a universal gripper that resembles a set of modified pliers.

Utensils are a matter of personal preference, but you probably actually require fewer than you think. When it comes to preparing food, you will need a sharp knife and a small plastic or nylon cutting board for peeling and slicing fresh fruit and vegetables. A can opener, pasta strainer, serving spoon, or spatula may also come in handy. If you can minimize dishes by eating right out of your cookware, each camper then needs only to claim a spoon for eating and perhaps, an insulated mug of his own. That last item can be very useful for everything from coffee and soup to oatmeal. If you'd like to allot yourself the luxury of a fork and a bowl of your own, please do—but camping does have a nice way of reminding you just how simple life can be!

A soft-sided collapsible cooler to use for transporting and short-term storage of perishables serves double duty as storage for the cooking utensils. Clockwise from the upper right, fuel funnel, sharp knife, waterproof matches, salt and pepper shaker, MSR pot handle, folded aluminum foil, plastic spoon and spatula, can opener, and cooler.

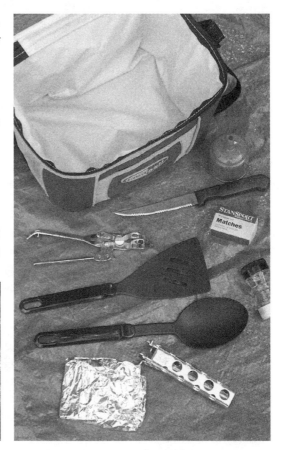

A collapsible kitchen sink and one-gallon water jug shown next to a tiny two-cup pot and knife for scale.

KITCHEN CHECKLIST

- ☐ Stove
- ☐ Fuel
- ☐ Extra fuel cartridge
- ☐ Stove lighter or wooden matches
- ☐ Pots and pans with lids
- ☐ Pot gripper
- ☐ Pasta strainer
- ☐ Can opener
- ☐ Serving spoon
- ☐ Spatula
- ☐ Sharp knife
- ☐ Cutting board
- ☐ Knife, spoon, fork
- ☐ Plate
- ☐ Bowl
- ☐ Insulated mug
- ☐ Tablecloth
- ☐ Tablecloth clips
- ☐ Scouring pad
- ☐ Dish soap
- ☐ Water carrier/container
- ☐ Aluminum foil
- ☐ Zip-lock bags
- ☐ Bear bag and line ■

Tina takes a break on a South Dakota camping trip.
Photo by Jim Woofter.

The old swimming hole at Rider's Roost is a great place to cool off on a hot summer's day.

Camp Clothing

Ordinarily, the choice of what clothing to wear while camping is not such a big deal. Maybe some of this and some of that or, as some do, a lot of this and a lot of that. Think it might rain or get cool? Well, better throw in some of the other, too. Since motorcycling will be a primary activity on any motorcycle camping trip, a good portion of anyone's clothing allotment will have to be suited to making your riding as comfortable and safe as possible. Beyond that, however, our luggage capacity is limited, and the dilemma becomes choosing clothes that are versatile enough to allow you to take part in all the other activities that could make up your ideal vacation: swimming, hiking, fishing, biking, sightseeing, or golf to name a few.

Weather can also be a huge variable, and it's always nice to be ready for every imaginable contingency—so as to be better prepared for the one you couldn't imagine! We've all heard stories of hapless campers being caught out, having to put on "everything they had" just to keep warm. Perhaps just as bad is arriving at your destination in the sweltering heat, only to discover that you have nothing to wear around town but leathers. And riding boots can be notoriously uncomfortable for walking. For years the only solution to this clothing dilemma has been either to do without, or find a way of packing more. For those who are willing to think differently about how they dress there are now alternatives.

Biker camaraderie at Mooney's Hog Farm ensures there are new friends to be met.
Photo by Jim Woofter

CLOTHING CHECKLIST

Your wardrobe, in addition to your riding gear, will vary according to your own tastes and needs, but to get an idea of what to take, here's a look at mine:

- ☐ 4 to 5 changes of undergarments
- ☐ 1 pair base-layer, long johns (top and bottom)
- ☐ 6 pairs of moisture-wicking socks
- ☐ 2 pairs of hiking socks
- ☐ 1 pair of khaki pants
- ☐ 6 tops (T-shirts, polo shirts, etc.)
- ☐ 1 long-sleeve fleece top
- ☐ 1 pair fleece bottoms
- ☐ 1 weather suit, jacket, and pants
- ☐ 1 pocket poncho
- ☐ 1 pair hiking boots
- ☐ 1 pair sneakers
- ☐ 1 pair water shoes or sport sandals
- ☐ 1 knit cap (for sleeping)
- ☐ 1 bathing suit ■

Bike camping doesn't have to mean full-time bike clothing. Biker clothing does have its place: leathers, heavy denier nylon, body armor, boots, and gloves are indispensable pieces of personal protection equipment for riding. But if your normal at-home clothing typically includes shorts, khakis, skirts, T-shirts, polo shirts, blouses, sneakers, and sandals, take them camping too. Not only will casual clothing open up opportunities for participating in many activities, it usually is more comfortable, lighter, and easier to pack. Lightweight clothing will also increase your ability to layer different items to fit changing temperatures and weather conditions, making your wardrobe infinitely more adaptable.

When choosing clothing for your outdoor wardrobe, utilize the concept of layering, whereby you add or remove thinner pieces of clothing to adjust the amount of insulation or ventilation you need to suit both the weather and your activity level. The innermost layer, or

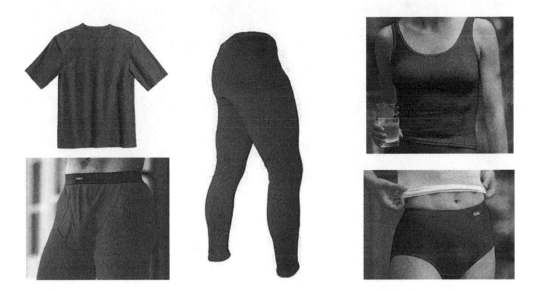

base layer, should be made of materials that help draw moisture away from your skin. Body moisture, if left undisturbed, will conduct heat away from your body core during periods of cold weather and, during hot weather, make you feel more miserable. The second or middle layer provides additional insulation and your outer layer keeps the elements out: wind, cold, and precipitation.

BASE LAYERS

The base layer you choose to wear next to your skin has a tremendous influence on how comfortable you will be in the long run. Damp drawers are the known cause of a common motorcycling complaint known as monkey butt, so named for the colorful posterior sported by the sore and afflicted. As long as under-gushies continue to be made of fabrics that act as sponges, like cotton and silk, they'll be wet and you'll be unhappy. The good news is that we no longer have to take this sitting down.

Enhance your riding and camping bottom line by investing in undergarments made from materials that help to transfer moisture from your skin, so you will be warmer in cold weather and more comfortable when it's hot. These new fabrics are at least partially hydrophobic, meaning they lack the ability to absorb water, so as a side benefit, your laundry will be almost dry after you rinse it out, meaning you might be able to carry fewer items.

~

Wool pants are more versatile than cotton twill and they're warmer in cold weather.

~

Convertible cargo pants are versatile and convenient.

Some of the current brand names of fabrics in this fast-changing field are Patagonia's Capilene, Dupont's CoolMax and Thermax, Duofold's Hydroduct and Hydrid Lightweight, and Terramar's EC2 Quick-Dri. You will find socks, boxers, briefs, bras, and undershirts (both crews and V-necks), in addition to many variations of the traditional long-johns, which, by the way, make especially good sleepwear when it's cool out. The good news is that these hi-tech performance undergarments are now readily available wherever sporting goods are sold and you might recognize these prominent brand names in the field: Under Armour, Ex Officio, Schampa, and Tilley.

PANTS AND SHORTS

Because blue jeans are already in everyone's closet, it's natural they should come to mind when selecting clothing to take camping. Bear in mind, though, jeans are heavy, bulky, and take up more room, proportionally, in precious cargo space than other options. And because jeans are cotton, they suck up moisture like a sponge, become uncomfortable and malodorous. If you must have them take just one pair.

Khaki cargo pants are a must have. Take one or two pair. They're light, comfortable, pack small, and look great. Hey, Indiana Jones wore them. A neat development is a cargo pant that, with the pull of a couple zippers, converts into shorts. How cool is that?

Unless you're ashamed of your legs take along a couple pairs of shorts. I've got chicken legs and I still wear them. They're comfortable and I don't care. On a hot day shorts are perfect in camp or while hiking, canoeing, or doing just about anything other than riding a motorcycle unless they're under riding pants.

~

Take two pair of red woolen long underwear. After a week rinse the first in a creek, river or lake and wear the other while the first dries.

~

Up the fashion ladder a rung or two is higher-end travel clothing. Travel Smith is one example of a company that has been around for quite awhile, specializing in high-quality casual and even dress-style trousers, shirts, and tops for travelers. Their clothing is extra soft and wrinkle-resistant even when packed. This clothing is not only great around camp, but it is also suitable for dinner in town at a nice restaurant.

SHIRTS AND TOPS

Even though we know there are many high-tech shirts and tops that meet the same criteria used to choose the foregoing garments, most of us are still unwilling to give up our favorite image-emblazoned cotton T-shirts, blouses, and polos for camping. Fine. Don't. But the next time you are shopping for camping clothes, consider the new types of travel clothing mentioned earlier that are made of modern, care-free, hydrophobic fibers. There are T-shirts, polo (golf) shirts, Hawaiian shirts, blouses, sweaters, tanks, blazers, skirts, and dresses, as well as the undergarments and pants already referred to. In short, you will find complete casual wardrobes for men and women that are light-weight, packable, wrinkle-resistant, and comfortable under a wide range of conditions. Meanwhile, if you must make do with your cottonwear, T-shirts and golf shirts pack up fine and will dry easily enough if wet, though you may need to take few more extras.

Aloha! A wide variety of clothing including pants, shirts, tops, skirts, and dresses are available in amazingly cool quick-dry fabrics. Photo by Marion Woofter

~

Snake bite medicine (whisky) has no place in camp. More trouble comes from it than from snakes.

~

FLEECE

Fleece is a polyester material that resembles a low-nap wool shearling. It traps insulating air well, making it the ideal fabric from which to make middle-layer garments, such as long-sleeved shirts and sweaters. Because of its amazingly high warmth-to-weight ratio, fleece can help to link all the lightweight items in your biking wardrobe into a functioning system that can meet the demands of fluctuating temperatures. Fleece can be worn over a base layer and under an outer layer, or in just about any combination you could come up with. It's available in a wide range of fabric weights and can even be bonded to other materials; its breathability also allows internal moisture to escape.

Riders whose camping may include cold days or nights should take one fleece top and full-length bottom. Fleece, along with microfiber underwear, is an exception to the rule that clothing should never be worn inside a sleeping bag. The reason is that these materials do not absorb perspiration but allow it to pass through.

WEATHER SUIT

When conditions turn nasty and wet, a weather suit is necessary to protect yourself and your clothes around camp, and your riding suit may be too bulky to do the job well. Motorcycling rainwear is usually not well-suited to hiking and other off-the-bike activities, so a lightweight, all-purpose weather suit can be just the ticket. First off, to do the job, a weather suit should keep water out during even the most persistent storms. Second, it must be breathable to prevent us from becoming soaked in our own perspiration. Thirdly, you should be able to make adjustments to accommodate changing temperatures. Lastly, ideal weather gear should also be lightweight and packable.

Garments that claim to meet all of these criteria are usually comprised of four layers. The first is an outer layer of tough nylon with a DWR (Durable Water Repellant coating) for repelling wind and rain while allowing moisture to escape. The second layer is a membrane of Gore-Tex or similar material which prevents any water which may have gotten through the first layer from getting inside, while at the same time allowing internal moisture vapor to evaporate. The third layer is open-mesh nylon that creates a layer of free space between the waterproof material and the wearer. This space is important for allowing the free movement of water vapor outward from the underlying layers. Your jacket also may have a removable fourth layer of Thinsulate or similar thermal material, though you can substitute other middle-layer garments. A hood is an especially nice feature, as hats really do little to keep water from running down your back.

TIP: Inexpensive, throw-away rain ponchos that come in tiny palm-size packages also have a place in your clothing kit. For day hikes, fishing, or a round of golf, they're just the thing when unexpected rain squalls occur.

A camp rain suit is made of fabric that breathes. Rain can't get in while internal moisture escapes. This type is not to be confused with a riding rain suit that is sealed, allowing no air movement either way. Photo by Tara Hartman

CLOTHES WASHING AND HYGIENE

Frankly speaking, clothes that are worn too long between washings or on hot days or under riding gear can, well, stink. No big deal if you never come in contact with other humans, but if that's not the case, then try to stay clean and stink-free. Remember, just because you can't smell yourself doesn't mean that others can't. This is not a small thing; indeed, there's one prominent motorcycle-only campground in the U.S. that refuses to admit riders that smell. Another problem with dirty laundry is where to stow it. Inside your tent? Packed away with clean stuff in your luggage? Wherever it is, it will impart its perfume to everything else. There are solutions. First, almost every community has coin laundries that welcome travelers. Second, most campgrounds also have laundry facilities. So for a few bucks each week, or as needed, all your clothing can be kept fresh and clean. A third solution that some use is just to dispose of soiled laundry, especially socks and underwear, and buy new replacements. Radical but it works.

Travelers should also be aware that the hi-tech microfiber items have had a reputation of taking on odors quicker than traditional materials and thus need cleaning more often. Clothing makers are now using special treatments on their fabrics to combat this problem. ∎

FOOTWEAR

Riding boots are specialty footwear engineered and manufactured to protect a motorcyclist's feet while riding. But riding boots are not intended for canoeing, walking for hours on concrete or pavement, hiking, or playing tennis. Begin at home by considering what you might do on the way to, from, and while at your destination, endeavoring to match footwear to the activity. For example, if the KOA at Kissimmee, Florida, is your destination and the itinerary entails spending all your time in Disney World, then the only shoes required (besides riding boots) will be a comfortable pair of walking shoes. Add golf shoes if a few holes at the Magic Kingdom golf course are in the offing and hiking boots if you plan on backpacking in the Smokey Mountains on the return trip. Since shoes can take up a fair amount of space in your luggage, try to choose versatile footwear that will give you the greatest number of options.

Lightweight hiking boots are made to be comfortable while providing support and protection while hiking. Photo courtesy of Vasque

HIKING BOOTS

The purpose of a hiking boot is to provide comfort, mobility, and maximum protection for a foot and ankle being exposed to the uniquely extreme stresses typical of hiking. Boots properly equipped for hiking protect the anklebones and soft tissues with specially designed support and bracing. They combine leather over-the-ankle tops, full-length lacing, and aggressive lug soles for secure, non-slip grip. Some boots have additional features, such as a waterproof Gore-Tex liner or integral ventilation panels. Lightweight day-hikers can also make nice all-around shoes for casual wear.

When shopping for hiking boots, try them on with the same socks you would wear in the field and give yourself adequate time to break them in before your first big hike. Most boots need to be treated in some way to improve their ability to resist water; follow the manufacturer's advice on how to best maintain your boots.

SNEAKERS

Many riders never leave home without sneakers. As soon as they arrive in camp or at a sightseeing venue that requires a lot of walking, the boots come off and the hot, tired feet go into sneakers. If sneakers are usually a versatile part of your normal wardrobe, why leave them at home? Some campers really like to get some regular exercise off their bike each day; specifically, a good pair of running shoes can give one the option of taking a nice jog.

~

Break in a new pair of boots by putting them on and then standing in cold water for at least a half hour every day and then wearing them until dry.

~

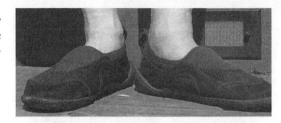

No fashion statement these, but these water shoes are great for watersports of all kinds as well as showering where so many have gone before.

WATER SHOES AND SANDALS

Looking a lot like rubber slippers, water shoes are intended to be worn while canoeing, wading, or swimming. You can also don them for bathing in campground shower houses, to keep things both simple and sanitary. Water shoes cost only a few bucks and take up very little space in your luggage. By the same token, athletic sandals are very popular among some crowds, both for the specific water activities described, and as casual wear in a wide rage of circumstances. They sometimes are worn with socks; although this combination may look a little strange to the uninitiated, it can make sandals so all-around practical that fans of it seem not to notice how funny they may look to the rest of us!

KNIT CAP

Cold sleepers will appreciate a knit cap since it's true that more heat is lost from the head than from other parts of the body and it's also true that cold feet may be warmed by wearing a hat. Many experienced campers always wear a knit hat at night.

SOCKS

Oh, happy feet. Feet that are hot and sweaty are not happy. They're uncomfortable, stinky, and subject to infestations too disgusting to mention. Feet that are hot and damp are also much more prone to blistering. Say goodbye forever to cotton socks and invest in a few

A long time coming, but now you can wear moisture-wicking socks for casual wear, too.

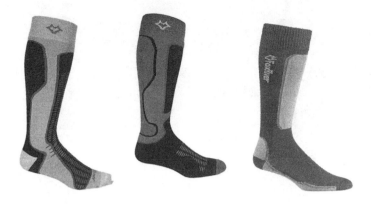

Yes, microfibers are woven into the moisture-wicking threads of riding socks now, making the socks comfortable in cooler and cold weather.

pair of hi-tech performance socks. What makes them high performance? They're made of materials or blends of materials that wick moisture away from your skin (keeping your feet dry) and they have engineered padding in all the right places to keep your feet cushioned and comfy. And because of their extra thickness, they won't wear as fast. Your investment will last a long time. Sport socks come in a wide variety of options including ankle lengths ranging from golf-anklets to high over-the-calf. The former are preferred mostly by runners while the latter are more frequently seen on alpine hikers. Their extra length is protection against scrapes and bruises. Standard crew-length socks will be the most practical as they can be worn for any application including riding.

A brief scan through the pages of an outdoor accessory catalog, such as Campmor, will reveal a mind-boggling array of materials used to make performance socks. There's wool and polyester, wool and nylon, wool and Coolmax, wool and Lycra, Coolmax and Lycra . . . get the picture? There's about every material and combination one can imagine. Which is better? Well, ask a half dozen experienced outdoorsmen and you'll get the proverbial six different answers. The fact is they're all very good. Furthermore you can take stock in the fact that they are all made by reputable companies and are being sold by a leading dealer with an excellent reputation. We haven't used them all, by any means, but have had good success with the hiking and walking socks of blended Coolmax, acrylic, nylon, and spandex by Thorlo.

All this comes at a cost as you might imagine so don't expect to pay two bucks a pair as you might for everyday socks at the Mart. The socks we use set us back $16 a pair but they're worth every penny.

~

Make your own boot leather waterproofing by mixing one part rosin with two parts beeswax and three parts of tallow.

~

Gale Schickel, owner of the Schickel Motorcycle Company, Stamford, Connecticut, set out on a coast to coast trip June 3, 1915. His camping trailer was a prairie schooner that tipped the scales at a mere 1,900 lbs! Photos courtesy of Ken Anderson.

Schickel's two sons rode a lightweight model equipped with a double, side-by-side, seat!

Trailers

A few years ago, on a trip westward from my home in Ohio to the Rocky Mountains, I began to notice that every service area, rest stop, exit and entrance ramp, motel, and restaurant was filled with motorcycles towing trailers. Popular sites like the Corn Palace, Badlands National Park, Mount Rushmore, Devils Tower, and, of course, the famous Wall Drug were overflowing with Gold Wing rigs with trailers color-matched to the bikes and helmets. What a splendid sight it was, a veritable moving rainbow stretching to their ultimate destination, a Honda rally in Montana.

Several days later while camping in Durango, Colorado, two couples riding a pair of Wings and towing "pop-up" camping trailers pulled into sites near ours, and I was astounded that it took but a few minutes to set up their camp completely, save for setting out the lawn chairs—no fussing around with tarps, lines, or mattresses. Needless to say, I was immediately sold on the practicality of these rigs. In a word, they are neat.

Bikers who use camping trailers often claim that their age or health would preclude their enjoying tent camping. Many people simply don't like sleeping "on the ground," preferring instead the convenience, comfort, and extra cargo space that a camper offers. Apparently there must be something to it, for this much is certain: very few riders, if any, go back to tent camping.

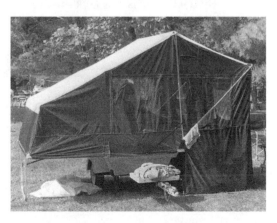

For many bikers, a camping trailer adds a touch of luxury.

A pair of "Wingers" use their trailer as a cargo hauler as well as a camper.

CAMPING TRAILERS

The basic mechanical concept of pop-up campers is a metal-framed, fabric-covered tent combined with an enclosed, two-wheeled trailer. When the latches are released, the hardtop either swings open or elevates vertically. The metal frame with the attached fabric cover then swings out and down to the ground to form the tent and enclosed vestibule. Except for a few minor adjustments, that's all there is to it.

Though the market for these campers is currently small, it is growing. You can readily obtain information about them by searching the web or by contacting dealers directly. Many dealers and manufacturers also exhibit at motorcycle rallies and trade shows where you can actually try out the beds and kick the tires.

Pop-up camping trailers may range in sleeping capacity from one to as many as six persons. The smallest model is a cute little number that's not much more than a cargo trailer with a clamshell lid and a tiny sleeping platform. The largest units have two platforms that support queen-sized beds! There are generally several options available, such as coolers and add-on rooms. Built-in vestibules may house dining tables, cooking paraphernalia, or extra sleeping cots, but for most campers, vestibules serve as screened porches in which to relax. Owners can further personalize their trailers with custom painting, chrome add-ons, and lighting options.

~

Sweet disposition, courteous behavior and a good sense of humor are the three most important things you can ever take to camp.

~

Patricia and Brian Savulis demonstrated setting up their camper at an Americade campground.

80 Seconds!

Compact and yet still roomy, this is a swell camper for two. Photo courtesy Roadman Campers

MANAGING THE EXTRA WEIGHT

One of the by-products of most camper trailer designs is lots of stowage space. Since the actual tent and frame mechanism are generally located above the trailer shell (but under the lid, of course), the shell frequently affords between 15 and 27 cubic feet of carrying space, for as much as 200 extra pounds of carrying capacity.

Balancing a trailer correctly for towing is very important, since a disproportionate amount of weight carried behind the trailer axle will translate into reduced or even upward forces at the hitch, making the back end of a motorcycle dangerously light. Conversely, too much weight in front of the axle will lift the front end of the bike. After loading a trailer but before hitching up, a rider should check the tongue weight with a common bathroom scale placed on the ground under the trailer tongue. Rest the tongue on top of a vertical 2 × 4 cut to a length that will allow the trailer to sit level. Luggage and gear inside the trailer can then be distributed to achieve the tongue weight recommended by the trailer manufacturer.

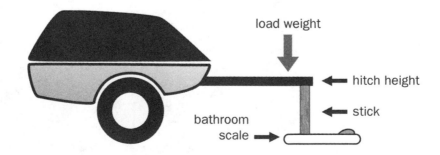

With plenty of storage room these cargo trailers are ready to roll.
Photo courtesy Roadman Campers

If the mention of weight raises concerns in your mind, it should. Having 400 to 550 pounds or more attached to the rear of your bike should give you pause, for it definitely has that effect on bike manufacturers. Every motorcycle manufacturer specifically warns against towing trailers of any kind and every motorcycle manufacturer warns of warranty cancellation if trailers are towed. They do not say why. You may surmise however, that at least part of their concern might be attributed to the additional wear and tear it places on brake and suspension components.

Is towing a trailer more likely to increase your chances of having a mishap? Not necessarily. Towing a trailer safely requires skill, knowledge, and even more attention than normal. I constantly (and alarmingly) hear riders state that they don't even know the trailer is back there when they're towing. It's alarming because that extra quarter of a ton that a trailer weighs will always affect one's stopping abilities, balance, and acceleration—in short, every facet of a bike's handling. And a rider who is lulled into complacency by a dull or familiar road may quickly find himself in serious trouble. Having said that, I also firmly believe that with due care, a rider may never experience any difficulties—and there are thousands of bike-trailer owners who would agree. My advice is to take it slow, ride a lot of practice miles without baggage or passenger, and gradually work up to heavier loads and passengers as your experience improves. And stay alert!

Since weight is the single most important factor affecting handling, how much is too much? There is no easy answer, but the general rule of thumb among trailer manufacturers is that a loaded trailer should not exceed 50 percent of a loaded bike's weight. For in-

~

First aid for anyone struck by lightning: continually splash cold water on the victim's face; if severe, use salt water.

~

If it's possible for cargo trailers to be sexy then I would give this one a "10."

~

Before you can learn to camp cook, you have to learn how to start and manage a fire.

~

stance, a bike weighing in at 1,200 pounds, including passengers, fuel, and gear, should not tow more than 600 pounds.

BRAKES?

What about trailer brakes? I've found absolutely no consensus on this one. Several trailer manufacturers told me that brakes are a matter of personal preference. Most offer electric brakes as an option, but none come as standard equipment. Rider's opinions are equally divided—they either swear by them, or at them. I believe the reason for the controversy has to do with the variability of the brakes themselves. The sensitivity of electric brakes, that is, how soon they become energized in a braking situation, is not fixed. Every time a rider departs on a trip, he must readjust this setting, as it will vary in relation to trailer load, road conditions, and the deceleration characteristics of the tow vehicle on that particular day (which in itself is a function of several factors, such as the conditions of the brakes and the weight of the bike). In other words, it takes some fiddling to get it right. And typically, throughout the course of a normal traveling day, these settings will need readjusting.

The goal of the rider is to achieve a setting where the trailer brakes do not come on until just after the bike begins to decelerate as a result of its own braking—and then with only just the right amount of force. If the trailer brakes come on too early the trailer will jerk backward on the bike. Even when the timing is correct, too much force may have the same result. Once properly adjusted, though, trailer brakes are a definite asset. They will keep the trailer from pushing the bike, especially during rapid deceleration, and will help prevent premature wearing of the bike's own brake components.

TRAILER MAINTENANCE

An area of concern for all types of trailers is the running gear. Tires, wheels, and bearings are exposed to unusual stresses; because of their small diameters, they rotate at a much higher rpm than the bike's tires. The consequently higher heat reduces the working life of the components and contributes to failures. On one summer trip west, I had three 12-inch tires fail due to heat. My advice is to always carry a mounted spare, a jack, and a grease gun with bearing lube.

CARGO TRAILERS

Most of the motorcycle trailers you see on the summer highways are not tent campers; the majority are cargo trailers. For many people, especially those traveling two-up, there simply is no other way to carry all the gear necessary for anything but a bare-bones camping trip, especially if you need to carry extra clothing for an extended tour or wish to prepare meals. A cargo trailer is a dandy option.

Most cargo and camper trailer bodies are molded from fiberglass, although a few are roto-molded using plastic compounds. Fiberglass has several advantages over other materials: it is incredibly strong; it is very light; and it takes painted finishes beautifully. Nasty extremes of weather and road conditions make it absolutely imperative that trailer tops close with a secure, watertight seal. To do this, they are usually equipped with heavy-duty hinges and locking mechanisms, as well as thick, custom-formed rubber gaskets. Underpinning the

Jim Knepp of Champion, Ohio, turned this car-topper into a cargo trailer. It's one of the best conversions I've seen. Photo by Jim Knepp

trailer boxes are A-frames of welded, rectangular, or square steel tubing. Suspension systems usually consist of either torsion bar or leaf springs and two 12- or 13-inch wheels.

The vital statistics of factory-made, two-wheeled cargo trailers can be summarized thus:

Empty weights: 125–185 pounds (without additional accessories)
Capacities: 15–27 cubic feet
Cargo weights: 200–350 pounds

For many riders, trailer bodies represent irresistible invitations for customizing. Many manufacturers have turned their stylists loose to incorporate innovative, streamlined designs, in addition to adding custom wheels, spoilers, airfoils, and swept-back fenders. Immaculate, multi-hued, gel-coat painted surfaces are the norm, as are chrome trim rails, rooftop luggage racks, and wheel covers. Interiors

Spotted a few years ago at Americade, this miniature horse trailer is the cutest cargo unit I've ever seen.

There is something about a Gold Wing and a matching trailer that just makes me smile.

are generally carpeted and frequently embellished at a customer's request with additional padding and lights. The end result is often a one-of-a-kind creation that belies its humble function.

Cargo trailers are usually lighter than camping trailers when fully loaded, so cargo trailers rarely have brakes, but you must still take care to distribute the weight evenly from side-to-side and as the manufacturer recommends.

Cargo trailers are incredibly popular, especially amongst luxo-touring campers. It's not hard to see why. The trailers make it possible for two-up riders to haul all their gear, and the weight advantage to the bike translates into confident handling. It's the good life on two wheels.

First, take a moment to catch your breath and calm down; there's no hurry. Switch off the engine, put the transmission in gear and/or block the rear wheel.

Second, bend your knees so your lower back is against the seat. Grasp the lower handgrip and the bottom of the seat rail or frame.

Next, with your back and arms straight, walk the bike up using small steps.

RIGHTING A FALLEN BIKE

When you find yourself in this situation, don't be too hard on yourself, as it surely will happen to you sooner or later. It's embarrassingly common for someone to drop a bike while trying to maneuver at walking speed, perhaps in a parking lot or at a campground. And if you're like the rest of us, your first reaction will be to look around in the hope that no one saw what happened—then you'll want to get the bike up and get away as quickly as possible, to save any remaining face. But take it from me—that can be easier said than done. If there is anyone around, don't be bashful about soliciting or accepting help; most witnesses are only too willing to lend a hand.

If there's no one around to help, however, all is not lost. Fortunately, as in many things, skill and technique can be as important as strength. I have seen both the methods described below demonstrated successfully by a hundred-pound lady with a heavy touring bike. Try practicing at home, on your lawn; it's a real confidence booster to know that you could get your bike up by yourself if you had to.

Before you attempt to pick up a downed bike, shut off the engine and put the transmission in gear or block the wheels so the bike cannot creep away from you as it is righted. Remove any extra luggage or gear that might make your motorcycle top heavy. If the bike is lying on its left side, put the kickstand down to prevent the bike from falling onto the opposite side as it's brought up. And lastly, turn the handlebars so that the lower grip is turned inward toward the gas tank as far as possible.

At this point, take a moment to notice how your motorcycle is oriented. Most bikes don't lie flat on the ground—footpegs, engine guards, saddlebags, and other bits will hold the machine up to varying degrees. Bikes angled like this are usually best righted with your rear-end against the bike. Back up to it and squat down so that your rear pockets are against the rider's seat. Grasp the lower handlebar with one hand, and with the other hand, grab a substantial piece of your frame, the bottom edge of the seat, or the passenger grab rail. This should be as near to your hip as possible. With your back erect and your arms straight, press back against the seat and slowly stand up using your thigh muscles, walking the bike up in baby steps, if necessary. If you're raising your bike from its right side, you have already taken the precaution of putting down your kickstand, so you needn't worry about the motorcycle flopping over onto its left. If raising the bike from the left, pause when the bike is just high enough, lower the kickstand into position with your right heel, then ease the bike down.

A fallen bike lying flat on the ground cannot be raised as easily using this technique, however, because you cannot get enough leverage from the rear-end position. Instead, after performing all the preliminary steps, squat down facing the bike and grasp the lower handlebar grip with both hands. With your feet firmly planted, back erect, and arms straight, slowly stand up using the strength of your legs. ■

When the bike is sufficiently upright, stop and lower the kickstand with the heel of your forward foot.

Then, gently lower the bike onto the kickstand.

Now you can relax after a job well done. Photos by Tara Hartman

Ron Smith has packing down to an art for two-up motorcycle camping.
Photo by Ron Smith

Now wait a minute, where do we put the rider? Photo by John Cheetham

Packing Up

Once you have gear and luggage chosen specifically with your intended needs in mind, all that remains is putting your plans in motion! Before you set out on an extended trek, however, you want to get familiar with the ins and outs of any new equipment before leaving home, setting up your tent, and lighting your stove. In addition, many tents need to have their exterior seams sealed before their initial use. Even when you and your gear are old friends, a preliminary working inspection should be a part of getting ready for a trip, to ensure that all your gear is complete and in good repair. A weekend camping trip to a local attraction can be a great test run to work out the bugs in your system before you take off far from home, to make sure that you are neither forgetting something important, nor carrying around a lot of extra stuff.

If you have not had much experience piloting a bike laden with luggage and gear, you should also give yourself some time to get used to the effect of the added load on your motorcycle's handling and suspension. A LOADED BIKE WILL BALANCE DIFFERENTLY. Slow-speed maneuvers can be especially worrisome until you gain confidence. Days or weeks before departing, load your bike, make the necessary adjustments, and get out on familiar roads to gain the

Loaded bikes handle much differently, and tank bags can alter the turning radius.

experience you will need. In addition, you should know that each year numerous motorcycle riders are injured—sometimes fatally— due to improperly loaded bikes. This should come as no surprise; summertime highways are replete with bikes that look like accidents waiting to happen—enough to indicate that many motorcyclists take load carrying all too casually. As a conscientious motorcyclist, you should be aware that there are safe ways to manage loads—and there are even more unsafe ways. It's your responsibility to know the difference and manage the risks that are under your control.

GETTING ORGANIZED

Camp stores sell tons of gear to people who have left things behind. Tent stakes are real hot sellers as are matches and lighters, batteries, can openers, and toiletries. As long as they're relatively innocent items such as these—inexpensive and easily replaced—there's little harm done. But what if this is not the case, what if the missing item is expensive or hard to find, like an air mattress valve cap, tent poles, or prescription medicine? It happens to everybody sooner or later. Checklists can really keep you on track and prevent your leaving something crucial behind. Sample checklists are included throughout this book to give you a start, and you can modify and add to the basic items to suit yourself.

Organizing your gear also has the added benefit of raising your QML (Quality of Motorcycle Life). When you really need it, you want to be able to locate things quickly and efficiently—money at toll gates, a rain suit during a sudden downpour, camping equipment af-

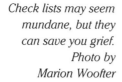

Check lists may seem mundane, but they can save you grief. Photo by Marion Woofter

ter dark, your camera for that quickly passing Kodak Moment. It often helps to break your checklists down into different categories, stowing related items together in a nylon stuff sack or similar pouch. There are many types and configurations of such items available today, and some include extra padding to protect fragile items, or compression straps to consolidate bulky things. Liner bags custom fit to the interior shape of your hard saddlebags can also make transferring gear from bike to tent a one-step process. And, it never hurts to take along several extra garbage bags, for isolating things like wet tents and dirty laundry from the rest of your stuff.

Exactly where you stow everything on your bike will become a matter of personal preference, but you want to strive for a system where everything should have a place and you should try to keep things in their places. Such a practice not only will keep your camp neater, it will make it more difficult to lose things in confusion.

BALANCING YOUR LOAD

Although most people understand that riding a motorcycle is a balancing act, few give much thought to how added weight affects things, especially when it is positioned away from a machine's center of gravity. For the sake of stability, your goal should be to concentrate as much weight as possible low on the bike—preferably at or below seat level. For this reason, saddlebags and gas-tank-mounted panniers are the best place for heavier items. Luggage that typically sits higher than your seat, such as tailpacks, trunks, and drybags, should hold lighter items.

~

Before parking your motorcycle for the night consider the relative ease or difficulty in moving it after a hard rain.

~

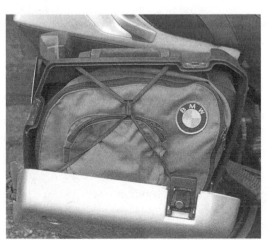

Custom fit trunk and saddlebag liners are the cat's meow.

Do-it-yourself luggage platforms run the risk of destabilizing bikes. The front of this bike will become dangerously light as gear is loaded onto this rear bread-tray-turned-carrier.

Although a top-heavy load can make a bike unwieldy, one which concentrates weight too far rearward will be just as much of a hazard, destabilizing the front end of your motorcycle and compromising your steering and braking. Resist the temptation to add large, home-made luggage platforms that stick out far behind the rear axle of your bike—they're an invitation to disaster. Balancing a motorcycle's load equally from side to side is also very important to the stability of your machine. When you are weighing your luggage on your bathroom scale to see that it doesn't exceed your bike's operating specs, check to see that you have distributed the weight evenly on both sides as well.

SECURING YOUR LUGGAGE

When it comes to securing your gear, the union of luggage and motorcycle is meant to be a lasting marriage—at least for as long as you are motoring down the road. But alas, vibration and wind are constantly trying to divorce panniers, saddlebags, tail trunks, and all else from the machine. The key to preventing this from happening is knowing the right way to attach luggage.

Hard luggage typically attaches to a bike via steel or aluminum brackets, nuts, and bolts to create an integral system that you would expect to be as secure as humanly and mechanically possible. But my own experience reflects the fact that it is not foolproof. During a recent pre-ride inspection, I discovered two of the bolts securing my tail trunk had worked loose. Visions of what could have resulted had it fallen off while riding were scary; at the very least, its contents, including a laptop computer, would have been ruined. I was also disappointed recently to find that one of the inexpensive extruded

THE FOLLOWING STORY IS TRUE

This true story was relayed to me for its educational value a few years ago by one of the parties involved. Names and locations have been changed to respect their privacy.

About ten years ago two friends, John and Zack, set out for what was to be a pleasant weekend camping trip into Sequoia National Forest in California. After several hours they finally entered the forest boundaries and began winding their way up through the thickly forested mountains. Zack, who was riding about 50 yards behind John, was later to report the weather was perfect and the road surprisingly free of traffic. Suddenly and without warning John's bike began to violently fishtail. Within seconds the bike started high-siding, and John, quickly separated from the bike, tumbled and bounced like a rag doll for another hundred feet before coming to a stop in the middle of the road.

Zack immediately threw in his clutch and clamped his brakes, slowing to a point where he could leap off his bike. Running toward John he barely noticed the surrounding road littered with shiny pieces of metal and plastic that was once his friend's motorcycle. His eyes focused on John who was limp, arms and legs twisted unnaturally and unmoving. Zack, afraid to move John's now helmetless head watched helplessly as blood ran from his friend's mouth, nose, and ears. But it was too late, John was dead and Zack could do nothing except hold his friend's hand until help arrived.

Paramedics later said John was probably killed instantly, never aware of the fate that had befallen him. Police, after later examining the scene, reported the cause of the crash was a locked-up rear wheel caused by a gear pack which had slipped down off the rear seat and into the wheel spokes. ■

plastic hinges on my new factory bags had cracked completely through. Had both bottom hinges fractured while riding, the contents would have instantly scattered on the road, creating quite a hazard. Neither story is that uncommon, unfortunately. As part of your pre-ride inspection, you should inspect your cases for cracks and make sure all latches and hinges function properly. Regularly check mounting nuts and bolts, tightening any that begin to work loose.

The classic "T" Bag style is hard to beat.

Securing soft luggage to a bike is a bit more complicated. Since motorcycles vary in almost every conceivable way, the difficulty lies in getting the luggage to stay where you want it. A bike with a deep, wide passenger seat will have a stable platform for luggage, where a narrow "shotgun" seat presents little support and a formidable challenge. It's little wonder then that most accidents resulting from improper loads involve soft luggage. Even when a load is tied down snugly, it may slide out of position, potentially becoming entangled with moving parts or causing fatal handling problems. The tie-down straps themselves also may contribute to the problem, as buckles and knots loosen or work free altogether, allowing the load to shift around. In addition, the loose ends of straps, cords, and ropes not properly secured can easily became entangled in a moving bike's wheels, drive chain, or other components—with catastrophic results.

Obviously, you need to make sure your load stays put, using additional strapping if necessary. If straps or cords are to be tied, use appropriate knots and back them up. Make sure buckles and shock cord ends are properly seated. And the loose ends of any strap, rope, or cord should be rolled up and secured with duct tape. Before setting off, test all your handiwork by trying to forcefully shift your load out of position from side to side and from front to back—and don't be gentle about it! If your bike moves before your load does, you're probably okay; if not, make adjustments. Note that everything can

~

A dull camp or pocket knife is more dangerous than a sharp one.

~

152

Frequently check and re-tighten all luggage straps.

and will continually loosen up as you travel, in spite of your best efforts at home. Regularly re-check everything at each stop along the way, just to be safe.

Since the first edition of this book, accounts of problems arising from the use of elastic or rubber bungee cords have been mounting. Indeed, one of my friends was completely blinded in one eye by a cord that came loose. Others report cords failing on the road and spilling cargo. As a result *Motorcycle Camping Made Easy* now recommends that straps, rather than elastic cords, be used at all times.

Tank bags are the biker's version of consoles, glove compartments, and map pockets.

PACKING UP FOR A SEVEN DAY TRIP

Many motorcycle camping virgins appreciate detailed information when it comes to packing a bike for a trip. This is understandable, as figuring out what to put where is intimidating the first time. In an effort to save hours of trial and error the following images illustrate how one rider packs up for a seven day, non-cooking trip. Disclaimer: understand that there are many right ways of packing; this is only one. You will develop your own with experience. Not shown is the riding suit and clothes for day one.

Note that the stove and pot are always taken along for morning coffee! Not shown are many small items such as camera, meds, ear plugs, flashlight, etc., that are stored in side pockets of the rear seat bag, tank bag, and the two ditty bags. Apologies to all lady riders for only mentioning men's wear. ■

1. Tail trunk top: Kermit chair, GSI table.

Tail trunk interior: paper towel, extra cord or rope, tool kit, Coleman lantern, cook stove, two gas canisters, small pot, folded mesh bag (for wet tent, tarp), ditty bag/insulated cooler #2.

2. Rear seat pack: sleeping bag, air mattress, ground tarp, tent, bathing suit, and ditty bag/insulated cooler #1.

3. Tankbag: fleece top, fleece bottoms, sweatshirt, bath towel, and knit hat.

4. Left side saddlebag: six tee shirts, one pair of jeans, six pairs of underwear, two pairs of riding underwear, six pairs of socks, and two pairs of shorts.

5. Right side saddlebag: riding rain suit, camp rain suit, waterproof riding overboots, watershoes, and sneakers.

Well-mannered campers respect each other's right to enjoy peace and quiet. Photo by Ron Smith

Cindy takes a time out to bring her travelogue up to date. Photo by Lorne Sokoloff

Camp Life

While we all seek opportunities to test our camping skills in challenging situations, most motorcyclists spend the majority of their time at "organized" facilities, where specific sites are maintained and assigned to travelers as they arrive. Your first responsibility upon landing at such a facility will be to locate the camp office and check in. Resist the urge to continue on into the camping area to "look around" even though there may not be anyone to stop you. In the interest of maintaining security for campers and their property, facility owners and managers like to know who's coming and going. In fact some camps have installed security gates or guards near their entrances. Most will be happy to let you look things over before registering, but they like you to ask first.

The registration procedure won't be much different from checking into a motel. Campgrounds, however, do not usually require credit cards or hefty cash deposits as some hotels do, nor do they put a block for what could be a large amount of money on your credit card . . . they're not worried you'll make off with the towels or the TV set. Most camps do require payment in advance though. You may also be given a map of the campground showing the location of all campsites, roads, and facilities, as well as a complimentary garbage bag or two along with disposal instructions.

Upon arriving at any campground always check in at the office first. Photo courtesy of Rider's Roost

Most commercial campgrounds such as those operated by KOA will have amenities including recreation facilities such as this swimming beach and picnic area.

If the campground is like most and accommodates travel trailers and motor homes, odds are there will be clearly designated and numbered campsite locations as opposed to the "open-field" camping system found at motorcycle-only facilities. You'll be assigned a site number just as if you were renting a motel room. However, unless the camp is nearing capacity, you may still have the opportunity to look over the open sites and choose the one you want. If this is not offered, and the assigned site is found to be objectionable, most facilities will allow you to move on request.

It's an unfortunate fact of life, but RVs—self-contained trailers, pick-up campers, pop-ups, and motor homes—outnumber tenters by a wide margin. But they also pay higher fees than tenters, and receive amenities such as leveled campsites with concrete picnic pads, fire rings, plus water, electric, and sewage hookups. RVers are usually awarded the most favorable sites in campgrounds while tenters are often shunted off to the outback. In most cases this will be no disad-

*The bike camping areas of motorcycle-only campgrounds as well as areas for tent camping at many of the larger commercial facilities tend to be informal and lack utility hook-ups, but that makes them less expensive, too.
Photo by Blake Smith*

vantage, but in many camps—even those charging high fees—sites designated for tenting may be remarkably bad, that is, next to railway tracks, garbage dumps, mosquito-infested water, or perhaps situated on low land prone to flooding. Remember, staying in an organized campground is no excuse to settle for an unsafe or substandard campsite. Exercise all the skills you would use if looking for a site in the wild.

SELECTING A CAMPSITE

Selecting the exact spot to set up a camp is one of the most important decisions you can make—whether you'll be sleeping in a tent, a pop-up trailer, or simply wrapped up in a tarp on the ground. Mother Nature is a lot more than just warm days and blue skies. She is also high winds, rainstorms, lightning, rickety old trees, unbearable heat, cold mornings, insects, and dozens of other phenomena that affect campers indiscriminately. A campsite in a glitzy campground with all the trimmings is just as outdoors—and vulnerable—as one that's in a National Forest or alongside a country lane. But regardless of where the camp may be, a skilled camper is able to assess the surroundings and anticipate eventualities to choose the best site possible.

The ideal campsite is flat and level. Just as you wouldn't sleep very well on a mattress that was lumpy, uneven, and had large voids, neither will you on lumpy, uneven ground. Though sleeping pads and air mattresses help smooth out irregular surfaces, they have their limits. Remember, the flat spot only needs to be as big as your tent's footprint; anything larger is nice but not required. Note that flat is not the same thing as level. (A ramped sidewalk is flat but not level.) Campsite surfaces are great if they're flat, but they don't have to be totally level. As long as you can orient your head higher than your feet, a slight-to-moderate slant is "sleepable" (like a canted hospital bed) and can even be an advantage for promoting the runoff of rainwater.

Typical campsite surface materials can include sand, dirt, grass, weeds, landscaping mulch, and pine needles. All of these are acceptable, but some are still more desirable than others if you are sleeping on the ground. Grass is ideal, as it provides some cushioning under your tent and it won't make such a mess if tracked inside the way sand, dirt, and mud can. Rock and concrete are to be avoided since they are pretty destructive to fabrics; wooden platforms can be a little

~

When hiking in snake country never step down on the immediate opposite side of a large rock or tree trunk as snakes resting underneath may be startled by your foot and strike. Instead, step onto the top of the rock or tree and step off as far away as possible.

~

better, but all three preclude the use of tent stakes. Some camp-grounds use layers of wood chips on their campsites generated by tree-trimming companies. This type of base is easy to smooth out and comfortable to sleep on, but often layered so deeply that it can't hold a tent stake well. Note that thick natural ground cover—leaves, pine needles, grass and plants—can hide all sorts of lurking irregularities like potholes, rocks, and roots. Before pitching your tent, carefully inspect the ground where your tent will be, either with your feet or on your hands and knees.

Avoid camping near standing water, as it provides the perfect environment for mosquitoes to thrive. Speaking of water, realize that bunking down next to a babbling stream can lead to a sleepless night if you aren't used to the noise. At night, lakes and rivers can also shed tons of moisture into the atmosphere creating thick blankets of fog, which linger for hours after sunrise. Waking up in a river valley where the sun slowly "burns" off the fog is a stunningly beautiful experience that almost defies description. Just be aware that your camp will need extra time to dry out before packing.

FLOOD HAZARDS

A campsite that's oriented badly with the surrounding geography can leave a camper literally up . . . er . . . down the creek. After concentrating so much effort and money on top-quality, water-resistant gear, it will all be for naught if you get flooded—a more common and dangerous occurrence than you might believe.

Campers generally have the right to inspect their designated site before paying. Care to set up your tent on this site?

The Flatland Flood

Quite possibly the last place you would ever expect to get into trouble with floodwater would be in the middle of a large expanse of flat land. But it is rare to find a large area of ground that is truly flat. During wet weather, entire sections, which may be only one or two inches lower than surrounding ground, can turn into large shallow lakes. You won't drown or be washed away, but an inch or two of water is enough to soak all your gear and leave you in a world of hurt. Stick to the high ground, especially if soaking rains have already saturated the ground and more rain is anticipated during your stay.

The Base-of-the-Hill Flood

Camping directly at the base of higher ground, even a small knoll, is never a good idea if there is any chance for wet weather. How far away from higher ground will be safe depends on a few things, principally the height of the ground and whether there is intervening drainage. Obviously if the ground rises only a few feet there's not much of a threat; there will be some runoff but probably not enough to cause problems. The higher the ground is, however, the greater the risk will be.

The Valley or Flash Flood

This is no kidding. I once stood in a small valley in southern Ohio that a few days previously had been swept by a flash flood. Several miles of trees, homes, and the many lives they represented had been devastated without warning. I have also witnessed the awesome power of a flash flood in the dry, flat desert of New Mexico—miles away from the mountains and the rain that were the source of the raging torrents. A wise camper needs to take this stuff seriously.

~

When climbing in snake country never put your hands where you can't see.

~

Typical of many semi-improved campsites, this Ohio state park campsite includes an individual blacktop parking area, picnic table, and fire ring, but no utility hook-ups.

Shaded campsites are generally the most popular. This area is typical of those at the BMW Finger Lakes Rally.

~

Camping with a companion is more fun than camping alone...

and safer too.

~

Desert flash floods can occur almost anytime, but during the summer, mountain rainfall—the source of the floodwaters—is common and very unpredictable. Never camp in low areas or desert washes, regardless of how old and dry they appear. Valley floods are more predictable, since one can better know how much and for how long it has been raining. To protect yourself, avoid valley lowlands when rain is predicted.

The Riverbank Variation

There are thousands of rivers throughout the country and hundreds of thousands of potential campsites along their banks. I have spent many glorious nights camped in sites such as these, serenaded by the sounds of gurgling water as I drifted off to sleep. But you must never forget that rivers can rise and fall quite a bit overnight, regardless of the weather you are experiencing where you are. Camping on a sandbar or beach may seem like just the thing, but you'd be safer pitching your site above any discernible high-water marks.

TREE HAZARDS

Despite any concerns, trees are a wonderful adjunct to camping, providing an ambiance like no other. Pines, spruces, and hemlocks will leave a springy carpet of needles onto which you can pitch your tent, and their aroma is wonderful. Not only will trees provide welcome shade for you, they reduce the amount of harmful ultraviolet light that your gear is exposed to, helping it to last longer. Trees also can be handy anchors for clotheslines, hammocks, and tarps.

But trees do have their downsides. Berries, fruit, and sap that fall from trees can stain your gear and mess up your bike. A really thick growth that does not let in enough sunlight will foster dampness and

The lunch counter, bar and camp store at Punkin Center Motorcycle Resort are very popular gathering areas.

the creatures that find that sort of setting opportune, such as mosquitos, mealy bugs, beetles, termites, and centipedes. Not only can hollow trees harbor camp pests like raccoons, skunks, opossums, badgers, bees, and hornets, but if they are structurally unsound, they could be a hazard in bad weather. In fact, let's not forget that the terms "widowmaker" and "deadfall" refer to hazards associated with trees. Widowmakers are old, weak trees just waiting for a good excuse to fall over—the next storm, a strong gust of wind, or maybe just the weight of a butterfly alighting. Deadfall refers to limbs or pieces of trees prone to the same problem. Before staking your claim to a spot, inspect the surrounding trees for signs of rot, hollow trunks, and dead limbs.

Also note that trees are excellent lightning rods and their roots, which in the case of most deciduous trees radiate from the base of the tree as far as the tree is tall, are efficient electrical conductors. Consequently, it's as dangerous to be standing under a tree as it is to be touching the trunk. Tragically, many people and livestock are killed each year for this reason.

To enjoy the many advantages of trees and minimize any potential hazards, avoid camping next to isolated trees which, by themselves, are easily susceptible to weather-related damage. A forest can actually be quite a safe place in a storm, as the many trees dissipate the threat of both wind damage and lightning strikes, as long as no one tree is significantly taller than any other.

TIP: Tree hazards such as those cited above are further proof of the wisdom of always using a full-length tent fly to help protect your tent canopy from tree residue, fecal matter from birds and insects that roost in the trees, as well as most falling limbs.

HAZARDS OF CIVILIZATION

Camping among fellow humanoids can have many benefits and pitfalls, but to make the most of your experience, you need to evaluate your surroundings just as you would in the wild. A campsite located too far from the nearest toilet or bathhouse can be inconvenient, especially in the middle of the night. However, being too close may subject you to unpleasant aromas as well as the constant sight and sound of others coming and going, maybe cutting across your site in the process. The same goes for campsites near the swimming pool, game room, camp store, or bandstand. Try to stay as far back from dirt or gravel roads as possible during dry weather since dust raised by passing traffic can settle on your camp.

Also, before you get settled in, check out your prospective neighbors. Remember that there will be no walls to screen out the objectionable behavior of others. The vast majority of campers are friendly, considerate, and sociable, but there are exceptions. Many—but not all—government campgrounds prohibit alcoholic beverages while most commercial camps do not.

Note also that most motor homes are equipped with electrical generators to power their internal systems in the event there is insufficient power available on site. Generators are noisy and impossible to

Everyone's your friend at a campground. Photo courtesy of Blue Ridge Motorcycle Campground

sleep next to. While most big-rig operators try to be considerate, there still may be times when their generators must run. If you think this may be a concern, move to another site. Other sites you may wish to avoid are those located near dumpsters or other garbage collection areas as they may attract nighttime visits of raccoons, opossums, skunks, bears, and early morning garbage trucks.

SETTING UP YOUR CAMP

Before unpacking a single item from your bike, decide how your camp will be oriented. Facing the door of your tent toward the east means you can enjoy the pleasant warmth of the early morning sun and it will help to dry out the interior of your tent before packing up. Next, thoroughly inspect the tent site for roots, rocks, sticks, and anything else that could damage your equipment; holes can be filled in with leaves, pine needles, or dirt. If you have packed up well, you will have stored your gear in the reverse order you will need it, so you can get to the most important items quickly, without digging through everything. Not only is this a good idea in general, just for the sake of being organized, it can become crucial when setting up efficiently is important, say when the weather is threatening or darkness is falling quickly.

Spread out your ground cloth and proceed to erect your tent as you have practiced at home. Drive tent stakes in at an angle, pulling everything out snugly, but not so tight that you're putting unnecessary stress on seams and stitching. Don't worry about trying to drive

~

Never climb up where you can't climb down.

~

165

First lay out your ground tarp exactly where the tent is to be erected

Next, some tents need stakes driven in, while others call for the poles. Follow the instructions written specifically for your tent.

Take care bending and installing the poles to avoid damage.

tent stakes in all the way; just make sure they're tight and won't come out. Despite your best care, tent stakes frequently break or are lost. For that reason there is hardly a camp store anywhere that doesn't sell replacements. However, it's still a good idea for you to have a couple spares of your own. The poles that accompany your tent are unique, easily damaged, and expensive to replace. Take care not to dent or ding the ends of the individual sections, or allow the sections to snap together; assemble poles gently. Your rain fly will go on next. Some campers go one step further and erect an inexpensive tarp over their tent, to further protect the fabric from the harmful effects of sunlight.

Finish setting up by inflating your sleeping pad or mattress and arranging it inside the tent, along with your sleeping bag and the re-

Using a tent fly makes good sense in any kind of weather.

Now it is time to install the fly stakes and guy lines to create the vestibule.

Finally, unpack your sleeping bag, mattress, and the rest of the gear from your bike in time for a well-deserved nap . . .
Photos by Tara Hartman

mainder of your gear. Never wear footwear into your tent; the dirt and grit will find its way throughout all your gear and can also cause serious abrasive damage to the tent floor. Because tents are small spaces, they easily can become a riot of confusion if you don't make an effort to keep things organized. Store all food items and containers outside your tent, in tree-hung bear bags, if necessary. When you are done, make sure you zip the screen door on your way out to keep insects from getting into your tent.

TIP: Leave shoes and other bulky items outside the tent but under the front and/or rear vestibule. Here they will be out of the weather but at the same time within easy reach—another convenience provided by tents equipped with full-length flies.

Big bikes, small bikes; you'll see them all when camping.

GETTING ALONG IN A PUBLIC CAMPGROUND

There are those who camp for the purpose of getting away from other human beings and those who camp for exactly the opposite reason, to enjoy the camaraderie of others with similar interests. Regardless of the motivation, it is a rare camper who never shares a night in the outdoors with others. Campers are not like a gathering of strangers in an airport waiting area or a crowd of people on a city street, all carefully avoiding eye contact and never conversing. Perhaps it's because there are so few campers compared to the overall population and that helps to create an instant bond between people who have never met—not unlike what happens between bikers. And so it's not surprising that, as with bikers, there is a unique, unwritten code of behavior among campers.

The first thing you will notice is that campers are friendly. They will actually look at you when walking by. Not only that, but most will speak to you in greeting, perhaps introducing themselves and striking up a conversation about your bike, origin, destination, or just about anything else. Don't be surprised at offers to help set up your camp, loan equipment or tools, or invitations to share meals or a cold drink. To fit in with this crowd, don't be a hermit—get out and meet people. It's quite common to see campers constantly strolling

Campfire gatherings spark lifelong memories. Photo courtesy of Blue Ridge Motorcycle Campground

Hammocks are great for basking in the spring sun after a hard day's ride. Photo courtesy of Willville Motorcycle Campground.

about. Not only is this a good way to stretch your legs after a long day on the road, it becomes a great opportunity to interact with others on just about any topic you like.

While most campers are outgoing, if not downright gregarious, they are at the same time respectful of another's right to privacy. Recognizing that tents are not soundproof, they will conscientiously restrain themselves from intruding on others with loud music, raucous behavior, or unwanted conversation, and you should do your part to keep the peace. It may seem corny, but among campers, everyone is given the benefit of the doubt and the Golden Rule is alive and well.

Just as the condition of a home or apartment is a reflection of its occupants, so too is a camp. Messy camps, typified by dirty dishes, open food and beverage containers, and general disorganization are bad news. Not only do they reflect badly on the owner, they are also more difficult to live in and their odors attract unwanted insects and animals. Keep your camp looking neat and clean at all times, disposing of trash as the campground operator requests. Never attempt to bury or burn trash or garbage; total combustion is impossible and the odor of burning garbage will attract camp pests.

SLEEPING COMFORTABLY

If you haven't yet spent much time camping, sleeping outside can sometimes take some getting used to. At the very least, you might sleep lighter until you get used to hearing the sounds common to the outdoor world, as well as those of nearby neighbors, considerate though they might be. The earplugs you wear on your motorcycle can sometimes come in handy, especially if there is an especially loud snorer in the area! If you are typically the offender, try to pitch your tent away from others or at least give neighbors fair warning.

When it comes to sleeping comfortably, you have hopefully already chosen a sleeping bag rated for a temperature suitable for not only the weather conditions you will face but also your individual metabolism, as some people naturally sleep more warmly or coldly than others; for more, see Chapter 5: Camping Gear. Since the ground is colder than your body, you should always use a cot, sleeping pad, or air mattress for both comfort and insulation. To improvise a pillow, fill a stuff sack with soft things and wrap it in a T-shirt or towel. Some sleeping bags actually come with fleece-lined stuff sacks that you can turn inside out for just this purpose! Before going to bed, make sure that any items you might need during the night, such as your eyeglasses and flashlight, are in a handy place.

If you are used to sleeping nude, don't stop just because you're camping. In fact, due to the way good-quality sleeping bags are designed, they function quite well with *au naturel* occupants. If this isn't your style, wearing undergarments of microfiber materials is fine as these will not trap body moisture. Again, cotton is not recommended. These items may also help your sleeping bag stay cleaner. If the bag is too warm, sleep with it partially or fully unzipped. Of course, cold weather is usually more of a concern than hot weather. Never wear day clothing to bed, even if microfiber, as these items will impart dirt and odors to your bag interior. If your bag sports such features, cinch up the neck collar and hood as your next line of defense.

If you think it's going to be cold out, do your best to go to bed clean, well-fed, and adequately hydrated. Some campers have been known to fill a leak-proof water bottle with hot water and stow it down by their feet.

COLD AND COOL NIGHT CAMPING

Near the top of the list of new-camper complaints is getting cold at night. Agreed. There's nothing nice about trying to sleep when cold. Adequate rest isn't possible while the body stays tense and the results are backaches and sore muscles the next day. Getting cold is a negative experience that leads many newcomers to swear off camping forever. Here are few proven tips for cold night camping:

- Use a sleeping bag that is made for 15 to 20 degrees (F) colder nighttime temperatures than forecasted.
- Cover the sleeping pad with an inexpensive "space blanket."
- Cover the top of the sleeping bag with another inexpensive "space blanket."

- Wear long fleece leggings and top to sleep in.
- Wear fleece socks.
- Wear a knit cap pulled down over your ears and the back of your neck.
- Tighten sleeping bag hood down over your head.
- Keep your arms and hands inside the bag while sleeping.
- Many experienced campers hang a candle lantern, equipped with reflector, inside the top, center of the tent. This produces a small amount of heat, but more importantly consumes the dampness resulting from moist human breath.
- Never burn a liquid or gas stove or gas heater in a tent.
- If electricity is available you may safely use a small ceramic space heater and ignore all of the above. However, use of older electric heaters with toaster-like coils is not recommended, as they may be fire hazards.

PERSONAL SECURITY

Although the incidence of campground crime is exceedingly rare, it is always wise to be smart, careful, and responsible, especially when you are interacting with a fairly transient crowd. Most travelers exercise some measure of caution without giving it a second thought, as a usual part of their road routine. There are all sorts of methods of securing your motorcycle, and you have probably already established a system comprised of disc locks, chains, and/or alarms that you are comfortable with. Another effective but inexpensive security device is a lightweight cover for your motorcycle. Not only will it keep your bike a lot cleaner in the woods, it can also hide a tempting display of dashboard electronics from passing view. When the weather is really foul, you can also use the extra space beneath your bike cover for stashing a bulky item, like your jacket, without giving up room inside your tent.

Cables are also useful for locking up a helmet and/or jacket if you are going to be away from your bike for a while. Many folks who spend several days in a base camp will routinely lock the zipper tabs

~

Never carve your initials into a live tree. Beside being illegal in government forests and parks, this exposes the tree to microscopic and larger pathogens and insects.

~

of their tent together with a little padlock before they leave for the day. Of course, this will not stop any determined thief, but it will deter a casual troublemaker and you will know if someone was tampering with your things while you were out. High-tensile steel cable nets are also available for enclosing backpacks, duffel bags, and piles of loose camping gear. If you typically use a money belt or neck wallet for those things you can least afford to lose, do not leave it hanging on a shower hook with your towel where someone could reach over the door and snatch both—an enterprising maneuver which can slow your pursuit just enough to secure the getaway!

It must be emphasized that while the above precautions are enumerated for those who need to know their options, I have no knowledge, personal or second-hand, of any incidence of theft in any campground or at any rally site.

One subject of conversation that often arises concerns firearms. Many bikers as well as many RVers (yes, those huge rigs that mom and pop use) are equipped with some form of firearm for personal protection both against would-be two-legged as well as four-legged threats. Motorcycle campers need to know that regulations concerning the carrying of firearms are set by individual states and vary accordingly. No state bans the carrying of arms in a vehicle or on a motorcycle but the ways and means vary. Websites such as NRA-ILA are useful for learning each state's regulations. Many states allow the carrying of concealed weapons on one's person. Campers should know that these laws also vary from state to state and usually affect the laws concerning carrying firearms in vehicles. States that allow a person to carry a concealed weapon often have reciprocal agreements with other states. This means that a carry permit issued in one state may also be valid in others. It's wise to do your homework in advance.

With few exceptions, carrying handguns into Canada is strictly prohibited. Travelers are warned never to approach the border gates with a handgun and then inquire about the legalities. By that time it's too late and you are in deep, deep trouble. Long guns are allowed in Canada (and recommended for those camping in bear country) but must first be approved by customs officials in the country of origin. Contact the Royal Canadian Mounted Police Firearms Center (www.rcmp.ca/cfp) to review all applicable rules and to obtain copies of required permit forms well in advance of your trip.

~

Enjoying camping as it is meant to be experienced means rising at dawn, enjoying the day then making camp well before dark.

~

STRIKING CAMP

In the morning, once you are sure you no longer need your tent fly for privacy, you should remove it and drape it upside down over the tent or clothes line for any condensation to dry while you are finishing your other chores. If you have the time, you could also air your sleeping bag a bit in a sunny spot before stuffing it into its sack. Free-standing tents can be overturned and brushed off, shaking out any dirt that may have found its way inside. Stow your gear in the reverse order you will need it if you were setting up: fly, stakes and lines, poles, tent, and groundsheet last. Remove any clotheslines and prepare to dispose of any trash as directed. Lastly, make a careful inspection of your site before you go, to be sure that you have not left anything behind accidentally, like a tent stake.

DEALING WITH RAIN

Rain is a fact of life when spending time outdoors. As a motorcyclist, you have probably already come to terms with this on some level! Even so, pitching a tent in the rain is not a particularly happy experience, but once it's up, things don't usually look so bad from that point onward. Of course, it will help if you are familiar with your equipment and can lay your hands on things quickly without having to unpack everything else first. Many tents need to have their exterior seams sealed before their initial use, and you want to have taken care of that before your trip.

When setting up your tent, pay particular attention to ground features that may spell flooding trouble. Assemble your poles first, and then get your tent up without delay, guying out your fly to best shed

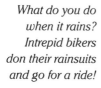

What do you do when it rains? Intrepid bikers don their rainsuits and go for a ride!

Wet tents will dry quickly in the wind when stashed on top in a mesh bag.

rain. Use a sponge or bandana to mop up any errant water inside your tent before moving the rest of your things inside. You may want to wait to unroll your bedding until some of the dampness has dried out. Believe it or not, the heat of your body will help to accomplish this. You can even string a little clothesline inside your tent to dry a few small things, such as a small towel or a pair of socks. Vestibules make a great place to stash raingear and muddy boots. A motorcycle cover will not only keep your bike nicer, it can give you an extra space to stash something bulky, such as your helmet or jacket.

When it comes to rolling vs. stuffing for short-term storage, the best advice is to roll a clean tent but stuff a dirty or wet tent. Sooner or later you'll have to break camp while your gear is wet, or worse, during a rainstorm. The best way of dealing with this eventuality is to stuff, not roll, the tent into a large sack, mesh if possible. This maximizes the free flow of air through the fabric and minimizes the risk of mildew. Keep wet things separated from your dry sleeping bags, clothing, and other gear. Given a chance, synthetic materials dry out quickly, so take advantage of any opportunity you get to spread these things out when you are stopped. If you know your tent is wet from the previous night, try to set up with enough time to let things dry out well before bedtime. Mesh bags containing wet tents can be lashed to the top of your load. A half hour or more of highway-speed winds will dry just about anything. Of course, you should always make sure a tent is put away clean and dry at the end of your trip, to avoid the destructive effects of mildew. For more on this, see Chapter 13: After the Trip.

~

If lost at night remember that the two stars marking the side of the big dipper's cup (opposite the handle) point almost directly toward the north star.

~

175

EXTRACURRICULAR ACTIVITIES

For many bikers, motorcycle camping means that riding is the biggest part of their trip, while for others, biking is merely a means of transportation to a camping opportunity. Regardless of which category you're in, there's a huge range of activities you can engage in off your bike as a natural extension of your enjoyment of the outdoors.

BICYCLING

True, you can't tote your bicycle on your motorcycle, but there are scads of campgrounds in every corner of the land that do rent both on and off-road bicycles and they will usually supply helmets, too.

BINGO

Not exactly high stakes gambling, but bingo, and other games, music, and dancing (round and square) are great ways for many to spend their leisure time while camping. Activities such as these are a common feature of many commercial campgrounds.

Making sawdust, as woodcarvers say, is a satisfying way of whiling away the time.

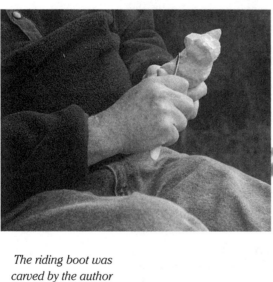

The riding boot was carved by the author and Chief Froggy by Sandy Wilkins.

BOATING AND SWIMMING

Canoeing and swimming are adjunct activities to many camp-grounds throughout the entire continent. There are camping areas in coastal areas that offer prime opportunities for both above- and below-water activities, such as SCUBA diving. Rafting is very popular in some areas.

ARTS AND CRAFTS

In response to popular demand, many public and private camp-grounds offer adult and children's classes in fine arts, theater, and all manner of crafts. These are great opportunities to show off your skills or learn a few new ones. The peaceful natural setting of many camp-grounds is also a perfect place for pursuing your own personal creative interest, be it drawing, painting, or photography.

HIKING, CLIMBING, ORIENTEERING

These activities are among the oldest traditionally associated with camping. Just pull on a pair of hiking boots and away you go. There's something for everyone, from short out-and-back day-hiking trips to multi-night backpacking ventures that require carrying food supplies and gear. For those not easily challenged there's mountain climbing. Orienteering challenges participants to find their way overland from one checkpoint to another with only the aid of a compass.

FISHING

Whether your angling choice is fly fishing, salt-water fishing, or fishing for freshwater bass, walleye, or salmon, you will have no difficulty finding a place to wet your line. If carrying your rod on a bike presents an insurmountable problem, either check out one of the fine collapsible rod-and-reel combos on the market, or rent equipment when you get there.

~

Trout can hear what you are saying so don't talk while fishing.

~

Trout or bass? Collapsible fishing rods will stow in just about any luggage and make for a great diversion.

READING AND WRITING

To many, reading is a fabulous pastime. Regardless of what else they may do on their camping trips, some people always find time for reading a good book. And you will have no excuse for not keeping up with your journal or sending postcards home telling everyone what a great time you're having.

SIGHTSEEING

Campgrounds and family-oriented attractions go together like peas and carrots. Like all the other travelers who hit the road, we roam to see different sights, experience new places, and take home unique memories. So after your camp is set up, hop on your bike, and go exploring!

OTHER ACTIVITIES

In addition to the activities listed, you will find many others offered—archery, shooting, hunting, horseback riding, gold prospecting, rock hounding, and volunteering for a variety of public and private conservation projects and archeological digs. To learn more, study campground directories and access public information websites, such as U.S. Fish and Wildlife Service (www.volunteers.fws.gov), U.S. Forest Service (www.fs.fed.us), and Wilderness Volunteers (www.wildernessvolunteers.fws.org).

NIGHTTIME PERSONAL NEEDS

This is one subject that other camping books tend to avoid but then readers are left wondering "What do I do in the middle of the night if I need to pee?" Your options are either hold it till morning, go in the tent, go outside, or trek to a bathroom. Here's how experienced campers handle it.

The easiest option is to go in the tent. No, not on the inside of the tent but in a makeshift toilet. First and always put on a light. You don't want to have any accidents at this point. For obvious reasons a small, hands-free, stand-up battery lantern works best. Males are fortunate in that they can simply unzip their sleeping bags, turn onto their side, and go into a wide mouthed bottle, jar, or cup. Females need to at least get up onto their knees to hold the wide mouth bottle, jar, or cup with one hand while, with the other hand, holding an inexpensive, reusable gadget specifically made for ladies. The device,

You don't need a fishing pole to fish, only a line and a hook.

178

With bikes and tents packed close together, walking around safely at night becomes a challenge.
Photo by Ron Smith

sold by Campmor is called the Freshette and is a funnel whose wide open end is shaped for the female anatomy. Extending from the bottom of this is a small tube that extends forward a few inches. Urine drains into the funnel then into the tube and finally into the jar. Reports are that it works great.

Handling the jars or bottles afterward is important but not difficult. If the container has a tightly fitting, leakproof lid it can just be screwed on and set aside either inside or just outside the tent under the vestibule for later disposal. Another option is to reach outside beyond the vestibule and empty the container onto the ground. There typically is 200cc (less than 1 cup) to 600cc (about 2 1/2 cup) and, because urine is sterile, there's no ecological disaster that requires Haz-Mat cleanup. In fact, unless the campsite is on concrete, blacktop, or the steel deck of an Alaskan State Ferry, it's immediately soaked up with no sign or odor remaining.

Alternatively, campers can answer nature's call, well, in nature. Finding a friendly tree, bush, or other secluded place has worked for tens of thousands of years and will work for many years to come.

The third option is to walk to the bathhouse, restroom, or toilet if the camping area is so equipped. Remember when going outside, unless there's a full moon and a lot of ambient light, take along a small light to illuminate the way. Tripping over tent guy lines is a common hazard, especially in rally camping areas.

The disadvantage of this last option is that it requires getting dressed and donning and removing shoes or boots and possibly jackets—in short, a lot of hassle.

The least acceptable way of dealing with nighttime needs is to do nothing and hold it until morning. For many folks this means little or no sleep. Waiting it out is miserable and leaves one tired and in a foul mood. Not recommended.

~

Washing your feet in cold water will make them tougher.

~

~

Experienced campers always wear hats.

~

STAYING IN TOUCH / DISPATCHES FROM THE ROAD

For the entire 20th century the predominant method used by travelers to stay in touch with the folks at home was the postcard. Today it seems incredulous that the tiny spaces on the back of these cards, hardly big enough for a half dozen sentences, would suffice to pass along information pertinent to health, current sights, itineraries, and so much more. Brevity was everything. In the days prior to television, color motion pictures, inexpensive magazines, and two cars in every garage, postcards were, for many, the only glimpse they would ever have of far-away sites and places. Picture cards were eagerly anticipated and rarely thrown away.

Alas picture postcards along with that era are quickly fading away. Instant, unlimited communications have, within the space of a few years, become the expected norm. Oral communication and text messaging via cell phones and "Blackberry"-like devices have all but entirely replaced the written message sent by postcards, letters, and telegrams, while instant digital images by cell phone and internet have replaced picture postcards. And why not? Why wait several days to weeks for a postcard message and lithograph of suspect color and bad resolution when the same image with superior color and detail can be sent within seconds from and to most locations around the world? Card collectors and my fellow philatelists bemoan the passing of the once loved instruments the way others pine for boat-tail speedsters and Victrolas, but rejoice in the higher value of their collections.

Film, too, is all but dead. The last rites are eminent. While, for the moment, it's still true that color slide film yields superior images for print media reproduction, the differences are almost indiscernible. For travelers the difference is far outweighed by the advantages that digital imaging affords.

In the space of time since the first edition of this book was written I would wager that the number of motorcycle campers equipped with cell phones and digital cameras has grown from less than half to near one hundred percent.

Taking photos on the road of interesting sites, landmarks, scenery, events, and people will never go out of style, but the method of getting them home has changed dramatically. The quickest, easiest way is by cell phone. While there may still be a phone or two left that does not have the capability to take and transmit images, most do. Now you can snap a picture of yourself with Grand Canyon in the background and send it to your guy or gal in seconds. Wow.

Be aware though that there are a few snags to be worked out. First, you may be in an area that does not have cell phone service—a "dead zone." Yes, there really are some places left that don't have the ubiquitous cell towers. Additionally, the resolution of cell phone images is quite limited. That means the images may not be clear, the color may be off, the consequent ability to reproduce the images onto hard copy prints will be limited, and just forget any idea of enlargements.

~

A dull ax is dangerous as it is prone to glancing off logs and perhaps into your leg.

~

Relaxing in camp after a great ride could be a great time to tell the folks back home what a great time you are having.

The best bet for the finest still images is a digital camera. Here are a few tips regarding digital cameras:

- Purchase a name brand camera from a reputable source. Avoid off brands from the corner convenience store.

- Name brand cameras with five or more megapixel resolution will take fine images.

- Always carry a spare, fully-charged battery.

- If possible buy a camera that uses standard batteries. Proprietary batteries are usually very expensive.

- Memory cards hold hundreds of images. A spare might be nice but really not necessary.

- Zoom lenses are a great selling point and many cameras are so equipped. This is up to you.

- Larger diameter lenses will take better images. Caution: Not the housing around the lens, but the lens itself.

- Buy a soft-sided case to store the camera and spare battery in when not in use.

When using any camera make sure to keep its strap attached to you. This will prevent damage from being dropped; you won't forget it somewhere, and it is far less likely to be stolen.

Now who doesn't have a digital camera? Snap off a picture or a hundred.

What to do with images once they are taken? You can keep them on your memory card and do nothing else until returning home or you can send them home now.

There are a few different methods of sending your images out to the world, to loved ones or friends. The easiest is via a cable from the camera into a computer and then attaching the images to an email sent through the Internet. This method takes but a few minutes to hook up and then barely seconds to send. Presto, your recipients receive great quality pictures. The magic word with this method is computer. With a laptop equipped with wireless Internet capability, you can visit a location that has wireless Internet service (wi-fi)—most libraries, large bookstores, coffee shops, and many national-chain fast food franchises. If they have it, it's free. If you aren't lugging a laptop around, many cities have locations where you can find computers you can use, sometimes for free, sometimes for a fee. Almost every library has computers that are usually free to use. And then there are so-called Internet cafés that also rent computers on site. The charge is usually a set fee for a fixed period of time, say 15 or 30 minutes. Make sure to shop around as the fees and time limits may vary widely.

Another way of sending images is by subscribing to a satellite Internet service. This allows linking up your laptop virtually anywhere the provider offers service; you may be in a city, in a campground, or on a mountain. Usually, if you have cell phone service it means the satellite will also hook up your computer. Now, this doesn't rely on or use a cell phone it's just an indicator of probable availability. This method is much easier to use than looking for a wi-fi location but it's also expensive and requires a monthly contract..

A last resort method of getting your images home ahead of you is to pop the memory card into an envelope and mail it. Just make sure you have a spare to use in its place.

~

Whole logs, whether small or large in diameter are the devil to burn. Split logs are tremendously easier. Quarter-split logs are the best.

~

MOTORCYCLES AND
THE GOLDEN AGE OF CAMPING

The Golden Age of Camping, that era when the outdoor sport that was uniquely European and North-American in origin, reached its zenith in popularity, began around the beginning of the 20th century. Prior to that, camping had largely been the domain of soldiers, trappers, cowboys, and explorers. For these folks, camping was not a sport but the necessary means of living while in the field. For the vast majority of everyone else the idea of leisure activities of any kind was rarely thought of. After all, this was before the era of the 40-hour workweek and paid vacations. The American West was still the scene of conflict and travel was relegated to steam trains, wagon trains, or horseback. City residents worked in shops, offices, or factories twelve to sixteen hours per day, six days a week while the rural population similarly toiled on farms. Life was all about subsisting and there was little time for playing.

For those whose jobs or duty required camping or for the fortunate adventuresome few whose wealth permitted such indulgences, camping was a crude affair absent the niceties that would come to be associated with the activity in future decades. Two examples illustrate the point. First, tents, if they existed at all, were frequently little more than a single large canvas tarp or two lean-tos tied together. Having no floors, occupants were afforded little protection from the elements and no protection at all from seeping rainwater, not to mention curious and sometimes dan-

Zoltán Sulkowsky travels with his sidecar-equipped Harley Davidson in French Indo-China (Later to become Viet Nam) on his round the world trek, circa 1932.

Like their predecessors, modern riders still get the urge to travel to far away places and even circumnavigate the globe.

gerous crawling and flying critters; second, eating meant either hunting and fishing each day or being provisioned by packhorses.

Camping's change in status from a necessary evil to an object of recreation was given a kick-start in 1872 when President Grant created Yellowstone National Park, the world's first national park. Forgetting for a moment that the only way of reaching the desolate region required several days of hard horseback riding over roadless mountains, the creation of this park was significant for two reasons; it recognized and preserved forever what is arguably the most well-loved park in the U.S. and it signaled a rising ground swell of public appreciation for all natural resources. For example, 1872 also saw the New York legislature budgeting funds for a study of the Adirondack region.

Subsequent to these and other similar official actions were well-publicized travelogues to the wilderness parks by noteworthy personages such as President Theodore Roosevelt's visit to Yellowstone in 1903. It didn't hurt either that Roosevelt, after becoming a hero of the Spanish American War followed by a much reported big game hunting trip to Africa, was the epitome of a "new" phenomenon in America, the sporting outdoorsman. And just as today when so many attempt to emulate those they admire, the much admired Roosevelt's eagerness for "roughing it" fanned the flames for camping and outdoor life. Suddenly everything "outdoors" was hot. Spurred by these and similar accounts outdoor magazines such as *Field And Stream* and *Sports Afield*, both still published today, gained enormously in popularity. Additionally, scads of books devoted to camping and living in the woods became instant hits. Most notable among them were the classics *The Book of Camping and Woodcraft* by Horace Kephart and *Woodcraft* by George Sears writing under the pen name Nessmuk. Both books are much-sought-after collectors' items today.

It was obvious by this point that the popularity of the outdoors was forever guaranteed but one minor problem remained—getting there. Not only were roads scarce by today's standards but virtually all rural roads were dirt and mud. Another obvious detriment to travel was that the horse and buggy were the standard of transportation in the early 1900s and the first generation of automobiles that arrived soon after were not much better. Fragile and unreliable, they were broken down more often than not. Within a few years cars became more reliable but at a price that few could afford. It wasn't until the introduction of Henry Ford's Model T in 1909 that things began to change. Here, at last, was a car that was dependable and, if not inexpensive, at least a lot less costly than anything else.

But man's urge to motorize and to experience the world's wonders was not tied to four wheels alone. The development of the internal combustion engine simultaneously spurred the imagination of tinkerers and bicycle manufacturers worldwide. They recognized that it was a lot easier to motorize two wheels, especially if the gadget already existed, than four. What followed was a veritable explosion of motorcycle marques, the likes of which the world has never seen. In the U.S. alone there were no less than 350 manufacturers and at least as many in Europe. The motorcycle's grand success, then as now, was thus credited to its wide availability and comparatively low cost. In an era before the world's economy would allow significant numbers of people to afford even a Model T, the motorcycle was truly the poor man's automobile. Further proof of this is that during the second decade of the new century fully 80 percent of new motorcycles were equipped with sidecars, according to the Antique Motorcycle Club. Sidecars permitted two and sometimes even more passengers and/or the hauling of camping gear, which in those days was quite heavy and bulky.

Thus did a symbiotic relationship develop that marked the fruition of the great camping era. Several factors combined to make this possible—the shortening of the work week and growth of leisure time, the ability of almost everyone to own their own car and/or motorcycle, the building of the national and state park system by the CCC prior to WW II, and the expansion of the national highway system (41,000 additional miles in the U.S.) after WW II.

With similar evolutions occurring in other countries, the urge to tour and to camp has grown exponentially. There is little doubt that more people are enjoying camping than ever before. The only unsettling news is that 2008 was the first post-WW II year to show a drop in attendance at some prime destinations in the U.S. Ominously, officials attributed the decline to children's preferences for the excitement of video games over touring and camping. ■

The Harley-Davidson
Enthusiast

June, 1923

This cover of
The Harley-Davidson
Enthusiast *magazine*
is testament to the
popularity of
motorcycle camping
in the 1920s.
Photo used with
permission from
Harley-Davidson

*Camping in Sturgis.
No, not South Dakota,
Sturgis, Michigan.*

*Camping in a Sturgis,
South Dakota pasture, 1994.
Photo by Ron Smith*

Is this where the "tent sale" is?

Camping Skills

Ah, for the good old days. Just consider waking up on a crisp morning during the Golden Age of camping a hundred years ago. First duty, of course, would be a visit to the latrine—perhaps a log slung horizontally over a shallow pit dug amid the brush some distance behind the camp. Toilet tissue? Don't be silly, there are plenty of leaves about for that. Then there's breakfast, at least after you catch it and clean it. Gee, I hope the fish are biting this morning. Your stove is a stone fire ring; the fuel is wood logs which you must gather by chopping wood in the forest with an axe. Matches too damp to light? Well, of course you know how to start a fire without them, don't you? With breakfast finally cooking in the heavy, cast-iron frying pan which you have backpacked over the trail, it's time to sit back for a moment in the log chair at the log table which you have made and plan the day's activities. After scrubbing the dirty breakfast dishes with sand at the river, and taking a quick bath there yourself, it would be wise to chop some more wood for the next night's campfire before going out on the trail to see if one of the deadfall traps has caught any rabbits for dinner.

Get the picture?

Today is tomorrow's good old days.

It is a hot ride on the back roads of the Navajo reservation in northeastern Arizona. Photo by Harlan Crouse

A well-known outdoorsman and writer of that era, Warren Miller, knew what he was talking about when, in 1915, he wrote in *Camp Life:* "Camping is hard work if you do it right." Well, we've come a long way, baby, and thank goodness. Thanks to the passage of almost a century and many concomitant technological developments in the camping equipment arena, camping no longer has to be hard work and a constant test of survival skills. Today, campers enjoy the privileges of leisure time and the opportunity to engage in a huge variety of activities while at the same time remaining aware that our natural resources are both limited and fragile. Although the list of skills a modern camper must learn is considerably shorter than it used to be, the satisfaction you will gain after mastering them will be ample reward for your efforts.

Always be aware of the potential of flash floods when camping in the west. Photo by Ken Gibson

Firewood must be split and dried before use. Even smaller logs burn better when split.

CAMPFIRES

Campfires may have begun as a necessity for our pioneering forefathers, but hundreds of years of art and literature depicting outdoor life have helped to maintain their traditional significance as part of the quintessential camping experience—even as times have changed. At the very least, modern land development and the booming popularity of camping means that we no longer enjoy seemingly unlimited supplies of firewood. Fortunately, the development of lightweight portable camp stoves and thermal-efficient clothing and sleeping bags means that campfires are no longer a survival requirement in the outdoors.

These days, indiscriminate campfires have really earned a bad rap for all fires. Not only can mismanaged campfires cause forest fires, campfire detritus left behind by slobs—ashes, half-burnt logs, blackened fire ring stones, melted plastic, trash and garbage—is ugly, harmful to the environment, and expensive to clean up. In addition, surrounding plant and animal life often suffer. It's not unusual to see large expanses of forest around campsites picked completely clean of every last log, limb, branch, and twig—no matter how small—and the ground pounded flat from camper after camper scouring the area for burnable material. These problems have become so serious in some areas that fires have been strictly curtailed or forbidden altogether.

Despite these concerns, properly managed fires—where permitted—are wonderful adjuncts to camping, drawing people like magnets to sit and watch the colorful flames pop, snap, and dance in the darkness, as the delicious aroma of burning logs wafts through the

~

Splitting logs requires an ax or hatchet. The longer the handle, the easier and safer the work.

~

Use caution when splitting your own wood. A slip of the ax may mean a very serious foot or leg wound.

~

A camper's tool kit should include a stone for sharpening axes and knives.

~

air. Nowhere except around a fire can travelers experience such a feeling of relaxation, contentment, and camaraderie, and truly know the meaning of the phrase, "It doesn't get any better than this." But keeping it as good as this for future campers means taking the time to learn how to build and manage a fire properly.

BUILDING A FIRE

The site for your campfire should be located well away from any surrounding flammable material. This should include avoiding the obvious, such as dry leaves, brush, and your tent, but remember, virtually anything organic will burn, including grass, mulch, and overhanging tree limbs. Even when grass and leaves are wet, the heat from a nearby fire can dry out things enough for them to ignite. Unless you are lucky enough to have a site of bare dirt at least six feet in diameter, clear away any flammable material you find within the radius of your fire. Never start a fire under overhanging tree limbs or within several feet of tree trunks, as radiating and rising heat can cause a lot of damage. Note any prevailing breezes that might carry off hot sparks and ashes and take steps to minimize any potential hazards. Additionally, a roaring blaze is almost always more welcome when it's located downwind from your tent, so you won't fill your home with smoke.

Most public and commercial campgrounds that permit campfires will provide a sturdy fire containment structure on each site. Make no attempt to move any of these unless specifically permitted, as the

Ideally, splits for kindling should be no larger in diameter than a silver dollar. Remember them?

earth below a used fire site is considered contaminated and moving the fire site will only spread the damage further. If there is no fireplace and burning is permitted you will have to build your own containment structure. The most common is a simple ring of stones large enough in diameter to completely enclose the intended fire and high enough that logs and hot coals can't easily fall out.

If you don't have stones at hand, you could build a mound fire. Spread out an empty plastic bag or piece of ground cloth over an area slightly larger than the site of your intended fire and cover it with a layer of soil or sand approximately four inches thick before proceeding to build your fire on top. The cloth and soil layer protects the surface below from heat, fire, and contamination.

FUEL

Open fires can suck up as much oxygen as they please, and that translates to faster burning and greater fuel consumption. One of those itty-bitty plastic-wrapped bundles of wood from a nearby service station or convenience store will barely get you started. Depending on the species of tree and dryness of the wood, a moderate campfire can easily consume a dozen or more large, split logs in two or three hours. Of course, in times past, campers simply cut their own wood from trees surrounding their camp, but you can imagine the devastation this would wreak today. Cutting standing trees, whether dead or alive, is illegal on public lands and is usually prohibited by

Food cooked over a campfire always tastes better than food cooked indoors.

~

owners of private or commercial property. You can usually use fallen, dead wood, but you should still ask for permission if you are on private or commercial land.

These days, the best way for you to obtain wood for your campfire will probably be to purchase it from a professional cutter who sells his wares nearby, often right at the camp office or store. Sometimes, a supplier will make regular rounds through a campground with a pick-up truck laden with wood, from which you can buy what you need. Once you have laid in a good supply of fuel, you will still have to ignite it, and for that you will need kindling—smaller pieces of split wood. To get the kindling burning you will need to use an even lighter, finer fire starter, which will ignite easily and burn fast and hot. Wadded up newspaper works great, as does clothes dryer lint mixed with candle wax or fine steel wool, either by itself or impregnated with beeswax. Pre-packaged fire starter briquettes are also available at most camp stores and work very well. Never use any kind of accelerant, such as charcoal lighter, kerosene, or gasoline in an attempt to start a fire! Not only do these liquids burn too fast to ignite wood, they are exceptionally dangerous and their use will mark you, in the eyes of expernieced campers, as a rank amateur.

Campers who have no experience with campfires frequently run into difficulty because they don't know enough about how wood burns. They become frustrated and leave behind ugly scenes characterized by logs that are partially burnt, or amazingly, long tree limbs, which they have attempted to burn from an end. Consider the following:

Different species of wood burn differently. Softwood, such as pines and spruces, are easy to light but they burn very fast and give off little heat. Hardwoods—oak and maple are two examples—are preferable. They are slower to ignite but burn slower and give off a lot of heat. Elm, another hardwood, is one example of a species that is notoriously hard to burn and should be avoided. Campers should be familiar with the different species of woods native to the area in which they will be camping before collecting or purchasing firewood.

Green wood—any species of wood that has not been cut into fireplace lengths and allowed to dry for at least a year—contains so much moisture that it will be difficult, if not impossible, to ignite and keep burning.

~

Fallen pine cones and pine needles, if not wet, make good fire kindling.

~

Building a campfire is not very difficult. It just takes a little practice. Start by concentrating your fire starter material in the center of the fire ring.

Kindling can be scrap lumber or dead, dry twigs. Stack it upright, teepee style, over the fire starter.

Light the fire starter at several places close to the ground.

As the kindling begins to burn, carefully add larger pieces against the stack.

Finally, add a few pieces of split, dried logs.

Slab wood —the discards "slabbed" off of logs at lumber mills—is lousy firewood since it is predominantly tree bark with a small amount of sapwood. Neither substance burns worth a hoot. Hardwoods, such as oak and maple burn well, burn longer, and yield more heat.

Wood that has been allowed to sit out too long unprotected from the elements will first dry out and then soak up moisture—eventually becoming too wet to burn.

Whole, unsplit logs, even when dry, can be extremely difficult to ignite and keep burning. If you must use unsplit logs, they should be no larger in diameter than your wrist. Splitting wood is not child's play. To do it properly you need a full-size axe, one or two steel wedges, and lots of experience. Not only is splitting wood hard work, it's also dangerous. A glancing blow or even a simple slip can result in serious lacerations or missing feet and toes.

Deadfall will not usually be found in lengths that will fit in your fire ring, which means you must either break it apart (much easier said than done) or cut it. Do not attempt to burn long pieces from the end. It just won't work.

AFTER THE FIRE

When you leave a campsite there should be no trace left of a camp-fire. Do not attempt to burn garbage, plastic, glass, foil, aluminum cans, magazines, synthetic fabrics, metal, or plywood in your camp-fires. Besides spreading odors that smell nasty and attract unwanted wildlife, all will leave remains that you must carry away. To reduce the amount of wood ash you will need to dispose of, continually push larger coals into the center of your main fire to burn as com-pletely as possible. After the ashes are cool, trowel them into a bag to carry out or to deposit in a designated receptacle. Removing ashes from an organized campground is generally not required. If stones were used to form a fire ring, scatter them as before and turn their blackened surfaces toward the ground.

KNIFE SHARPENING BASICS

Experienced campers know the value of a sharp knife; they also know a dull knife is more dangerous than a sharp one. Here's how to keep a keen edge on yours.

Use a sharpening stone only if the knife is really dull or has nicks in the edge; otherwise go right to the strop. Use a medium brown sharpening stone about 8 inches or more in length and a couple inches wide. Wet the surface with a light oil such as sewing machine or "3-in-1" oil. This makes sharpening easier and floats away fine particles of steel.

The correct sharpening angle is set with the edge flat on the stone and the rear held one dime to one nickel thickness high. With moderate downward pressure pull the knife toward you, with the edge leading. Repeat four times before reversing to the other side of the blade and repeating. Continue until nicks are gone.

DO NOT RUN YOUR FINGER ALONG THE BLADE TO TEST FOR SHARPNESS.

Stropping is the process of honing a knife edge. Most of the time stropping and not stoning is all that's required to maintain a sharp blade as long as it's done frequently. *There is no such thing as honing too frequently.*

Honing may be done with a leather mounted on a board or with the back (rough) side of a piece of thin cardboard like the kind that comes with new shirts. The important thing is to keep the material dead flat.

A dusting of honing (diamond) powder worked into the strop with a fingertip provides the abrasive needed to work the steel edge and impart a nice polish.

Hold the blade at a slight angle, as on the stone, but this time move the blade edge away from yourself. Never move the blade edge into the strop.

That's it! You now have a sharp knife again. ■

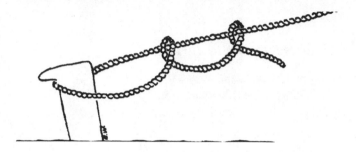

Half hitches, used in twos, are great for quickly securing guy lines around tent stakes.

KNOTS

Another skill from the past that is still frequently called upon is knot tying. In the halcyon days of camping, outdoorsman used knots for everything from lashing loads to pack animals and constructing camp lodgings to performing a myriad of daily chores. Blessedly, today's campers usually have simpler tasks at hand, such as tying down a tent fly or securing a hammock. Knowing how to do it right makes all the difference. The right knot will neither loosen during the night, nor have to be cut in the morning because it has become impossible to undo.

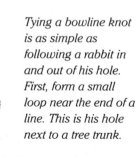

Tying a bowline knot is as simple as following a rabbit in and out of his hole. First, form a small loop near the end of a line. This is his hole next to a tree trunk.

Imagine the end of the rope is the rabbit coming up out of his hole.

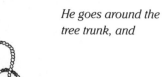

He goes around the tree trunk, and

then back down into his hole. That's it! Just tighten it up and you are finished.

A clove hitch is strong, reliable, and easy to untie. Practice tying all these knots with a length of soft rope until it becomes second nature.

From the vast lexicon of knots, there are three that will stand a camper in good stead for just about any task he is likely to encounter: the bowline, half hitch, and clove hitch. The bowline is arguably the most famous knot of all; certainly it is the most commonly used knot on sailing ships and is also frequently used by rescue squads. This knot is strong, easy to tie, and because it doesn't jam, it is easy to untie. It's a great knot to use on a line when towing someone out of a ditch or whenever a secure loop is required. The half hitch is a snap for securing tent or canopy guy lines. For maximum security, it's recommended that two (never more) half hitches be used in tandem. I also use this knot when tying luggage lines and securing the ends of webbing straps on my bike. The disadvantage of this knot is that it can jam under load and can, therefore, be a bear to untie, especially if wet. A clove hitch, though it doesn't have the appearance of a knot, can hold an incredible amount of weight without slipping. As a former urban tree surgeon, I used the clove hitch exclusively when piecing down logs and limbs weighing hundreds of pounds over residential rooftops. It's easy to tie, doesn't jam, and is just the knot for hanging a hammock or clothesline. With a three-foot long piece of practice rope and the accompanying diagrams you'll become an expert in no time.

A clove hitch works well for securing hammocks and clotheslines.

LEAVE NO TRACE

Recognizing that our outdoor resources are both limited and fragile, and actually doing something about it, outdoorsmen have adopted the philosophy of Leave No Trace, an ethic that recognizes our right to use the land, but in a way that assures it will be preserved—as is—for future generations to enjoy. Most of the actual practice of this involves planning ahead and preparing in advance so that you can minimize the amount of impact you will ultimately have on the land.

For example, you can minimize your use of open fires (and all the ecological downsides that go along with them) by carrying a camp stove and sufficient fuel for cooking, as well as adequate clothing and sleeping bags for personal warmth. By repackaging your food items to reusable plastic containers and zip-lock bags, you will reduce the amount of trash you will generate in the backcountry, and hence, have to deal with. In addition, you should take the time to get to know the rules and regulations of the area you will be in. They exist for good reason, perhaps in response to past abuses or current conditions you may not be aware of.

Leave No Trace means literally just that—when we leave, there should be no evidence of our having passed that way. It is a tall order, but not an impossible one if you can abide by the following guidelines:

Camp on Durable Surfaces

Soil compaction is a serious and growing cause of soil erosion, and accompanying loss of vegetation and biological habitat. To minimize soil compaction around campsites, park bikes in the same spot and resist the temptation to ride around the site or off-road unless specifically permitted. When camping in a well-used area minimize the spread of compaction by camping in a previously used spot. If the area is new to campers, or has only been lightly used, choose a

~

The meat of poisonous snakes is safe to eat.

~

200

new spot and shift your tent daily to another. When hiking or riding, use existing trails, don't make your own shortcuts, and if the trail is muddy, go through the muddy spot rather than around it, which would only serve to broaden the damage.

Pack It In, Pack It Out

Simply put, this means if it wasn't there when you arrived, take it with you when you leave. And don't be afraid to take someone else's trash either! When hiking, always carry along a small plastic bag to collect trailside trash left by other slobs. According to government studies, discarded paper may last as long as four weeks in the open, a cigarette butt 2–5 years, a plastic bottle 20–30 years, tin cans 80–100 years, aluminum cans 200–400 years, a plastic six-pack holder 450 years, and glass bottles indefinitely!

Properly Dispose of Waste

Do not attempt to bury or burn trash. To begin with, complete and total incineration is almost impossible in an outdoor fire and then there are the ashes to deal with at the end. Burning and/or burying also spread food odors that attract bears, raccoons, and other potentially disagreeable animals. Take your trash home with you or dispose of it in a designated location. Human fecal matter should be buried in holes at least 6–8 inches deep located 200 or more feet away from water. Because toilet tissue attracts animals who will often dig it up and spread it around, either take out used tissue with you or use a biodegradable variety available from RV dealers. Never bury or leave feminine hygiene products, containers, or plastic bits. Of course, this also applies to condoms and their packaging—carry them out.

Leave What You Find

Or, as it is commonly put, "Leave only footprints, take only pictures." Don't take fossils, artifacts, petrified wood, or other souvenirs from the natural environment. Besides being illegal on public lands, removing them prevents others from their enjoyment. Don't try to "improve" a campsite in any way by moving boulders, constructing log furniture, or pounding nails into trees. Never leave cords or rope tied around tree trunks, which could girdle and kill them over time. Unless the site is in an organized campground, scatter fire ring stones before leaving and replace twigs, branches, or other materials that you may have moved when you were pitching your tent. Leave everything as it was before you arrived.

~

For camp furniture use green or fresh cut trees rather than old logs. Also, pine is easier to work than hardwood.

~

Campgrounds like Bear Run are great places to meet up with a few friends. Photo by Ron Smith

This campsite in Moab, Utah, had a roof for the picnic table. Photo by Ken Gibson

Camp Cooking the Modern Way

One problem area that some motorcyclists encounter when embracing camping is in the food preparation department. Despite the amount of cooking gear sold by outfitters, some of it hardly gets used. In fact the questions most frequently asked at the many camping seminars I have conducted at motorcycle rallies concern cooking gear. I suspect that for many of those asking, their cooking experience is limited to opening a pizza box and a can of beer. Having seen the effort that goes into preparing a fancy meal they have shied away from even learning the basics.

Let me put some of those fears to rest. With the availability of many prepackaged prepared foods in your local supermarket, camp cooking can be easy, quick, painless, and inexpensive. If you can successfully change your bike's oil following the manufacturer's instructions, you can prepare a tasty camp meal following the instructions on the package.

Think of it, camp-prepared meals that are as good as restaurant alternatives—in much less time and for less money. I'm not talkin' beans and weenies either. But before we get ahead of ourselves, the kitchen needs to be set up.

Camp cooking is not difficult to master. With so many prepackaged prepared foods available it can be as easy as boiling water. Photo by Linda Knepp

Tablecloths are not just for show; they keep the crawly critters out of the food and the food out of the dirt.

With a few exceptions, cowboy cooking over an open campfire has become a thing of the past. Not only did it deplete popular camping spots of all available fuel within range, it was an admittedly messy and complicated method for reliably putting out hot meals. Fortunately, the compact camping stoves discussed in the gear section earlier all but eliminate these complaints. However, only use a camping stove in a well-ventilated space, and never ever inside a tent! If you've done the correct thing and purchased a tent with a full-length fly and at least one vestibule, the stove may be set up there during wet weather while you stay dry and snug inside the tent. Experienced campers have done this a lot.

SETTING UP YOUR KITCHEN

Before unpacking any cooking gear from your bike, check out the placement of the picnic table. If one is not available, clear away at least a three-foot-square area on the ground. A section of tarp may also be laid out in the interest of keeping things clean. In any case, much of the following is applicable for a ground site as well as a table. If you have a choice, opt for a shady spot rather than a sunny one. Some campers will rig an extra tarp high over their cooking area for a little protection from the elements. Next, make sure your table is level; put shims of wood or stone under any wobbly corners. Many of the wooden picnic tables you'll run across will be well-used items with graffiti-carved surfaces that have been soaking up weather and germs for years. An inexpensive, heavy vinyl tablecloth held in place with table clips will hide a multitude of sins, and keep everything a little more sanitary. Some campgrounds have started to use durable concrete picnic tables to deter table rustling, vandalism, and general wear and tear, but a tablecloth is still a good idea.

If there's a breeze, set up your kitchen at the downwind end of your table to keep from smoking out your guests. The stove is often set at the very end of the table, so you can stand and move around it freely as you prepare dinner. Arrange your food prep area right behind it, and set your cleanup basins and extra food and water on the benches on either side. Plastic pot scrubbers are ideal for camp clean-up, as they don't stay wet and smelly the way a sponge can. Another trick is to carry a steel-wool soap pad, but instead of using it whole until it becomes a sodden rusty wad, tear off a small piece each time you do dishes until it is completely used up.

After every meal, wash, dry, and stow away all pots, pans, and dishes, and wipe off your table top or cloth. If you reduce the amount of food residue left lying about, you'll have fewer problems with bees, ants, wasps, and larger four-legged critters. Remember, nocturnal mice, raccoons, and skunks will chew through packs and gear looking for edibles. If you are in bear country, follow local advice regarding hanging or storing your food. For more about dealing with camp pests, see Chapter 12: Dealing with Beasties. Finally, pick up all signs of garbage and refuse around your camp and dispose of it properly or carry it out with you.

CAMPING FOOD

Motorcycle campers who desired to provide their own meals have always been constrained by limited carrying space on their bikes as well as the difficulty of storing perishables such as meat and dairy products. The result has been a menu that is often lousy by most standards. One alternative is to shop for food supplies each day as needed. This solves the problem of preserving perishable foods but forces severe limitations on routes and timetables. Dehydrating perishables at home for later reconstitution is another option, though this, too, has its problems. The process is long, consumes a lot of electricity, and is most successful with only fruits and vegetables. Dehydrating meat is tricky at best and at worst potentially dangerous. It's also pretty much limited to ground beef. Forget chicken with its extreme risk of salmonella; fish is also troublesome. Of course there were always WWII "K" rations or the modern version of GI fare, the MRE (meals, ready to eat).

~

Here's a great way of making biscuits without an oven: make up a stiffer than usual batch of dough and after forming it into a long, thick strip wrap it around a long stick. Hold it over a fire and turn until cooked all the way around. Break off pieces to eat.

~

Unheard of just a few years ago, fully-cooked fresh meats needing no refrigeration are now available at grocery stores.

A few years ago another much better alternative for hungry campers came on the scene as a result of the U.S. space program. Now a whole new industry of dehydrated, freeze-dried, and newer yet, vacuum sealed foods exists. Due to the similarity of requirements and constraints between astronauts and bikers, these new foods are well-suited to the motorcycle camper. Today, there are numerous companies that specialize in freeze-dried gourmet meals hermetically sealed in lightweight, flexible, waterproof packages; preparation usually requires little more than boiling water. Primarily intended for backpackers and mountain climbers, these meals don't require refrigeration. A mind-boggling array of choices is available: breakfast entrees of eggs and bacon and cheese omelets, and dinner selections of pasta primavera, beef stroganoff, honey mustard chicken, Thai shrimp, black bean tamale pie, and hundreds (that's right, hundreds) more. Because they appeal to such a specialized market, you will find them sold through major retail outfitters, such as Gander Mountain and Cabelas, as well as websites such as Campmor and many catalogs that cater to outdoorsmen.

The one and only drawback to dehydrated, freeze-dried meals has been their price. At this writing the average price per entrée (almost competitive with restaurant prices) may prohibit cost-conscious campers from using them more than just occasionally.

Vacuum-sealed foods are different. This process allows meat and other foods to be fully cooked, packaged, and stored without refrigeration. Since the foods have not been dehydrated, re-hydration is not necessary. The best part is, when manufactured and marketed by large brands, the economics of scale allow the entrées to be priced amazingly low.

Modern grocery stores have an ever-growing selection of items ideal for motorcycle camping.

The significance of vacuum-sealed and freeze-dried foods, despite the issue of the cost, on campers and the general public will be (forgive the pun) astronomical. A survey of any major grocer's shelves reveals an explosion of items that is just a prequel to what will follow. Utilizing these items, the seven-day menu has been designed and tested (see page 213).

This menu is ideal for motorcyclists for a number of reasons, not the least of which is that nothing requires refrigeration. Because the perishable items have been fully cooked and sealed they can be carried without fear of spoilage. Notice the variety of dinner entrées; one of the major complaints of campers previously was the food was boring and repetitive. It is now possible to have main dishes that wouldn't have been conceivable on the road before due to the sheer number of different ingredients.

Everything in the sample seven-day menu can be purchased from your local grocery store except for the Mountain House dehydrated eggs and bacon, beef stew, and ice cream, which are available from outdoor gear suppliers. Most of the items, such as the powdered drinks, snack bars, tortillas, and dehydrated mashed potatoes, are available from a variety of brands. A few brand-specific ingredients included in the sample menu are Panni potato pancake mix, Oscar Mayer fully-cooked bacon, and Betty Crocker hash browns for the breakfasts, Lipton Cup-a-Soup, Kraft macaroni and cheese, and Bear Creek Country Kitchen chili for the lunches, and StarKist yellowfin tuna fillets, Zatarain blackened chicken with yellow rice, and New Orleans-style red beans and rice for dinner selections.

TIP: Take along a couple sealable food containers for leftovers. (You can snack on them later in the day or the next day.) Do not throw leftovers on the ground as they will attract unwanted visitors, if not while you're there, then for those that follow you.

~

Prevent ants from getting into your food boxes by pasting strips of flypaper around the outside.

~

TIP: A small, soft-sided zip top cooler is a necessity on a road trip. With it you can stop at roadside farm markets or a handy grocery for fresh fruit and vegetables to supplement the menu.

FOOD PACKING SYSTEM

Because a whole lot of items go into a multi-day menu, a luggage tsunami is imminent unless a good food packing system is in play. The most important rule is to keep anything related to food and food preparation in its own luggage. Mixing it with other gear is an invitation to disaster. Food packages can get ripped open by jostling with other items. Not only will the food item be ruined but it may take days to get everything else cleaned up.

An even more important reason to have a food packing system is that it will save eons of time. Time otherwise spent searching through the entire food supply for an item, or two, or three. And then repeated several times a day and then day after day. Get the picture?

Whether or not you use the sample menu provided, begin with a written menu. This saves a lot of time and money in the grocery store stocking up, as it prevents forgetting necessary items, and it forestalls buying items you don't need. Buy several sizes of good quality, clear, food storage bags. The ones with zippers work best for this.

With menu, food, and bags in hand, stow every food item for each meal in its own bag. Do this for every meal of the trip. Breakfasts, snacks, and some lunches will fit in the smallest of the bags. Dinners will fit into the medium-sized bags. Remember to include every item for each particular meal. This includes small items like condiments, salt, pepper, coffee creamer, and sweetener.

First put each meal and each snack into its own bag.

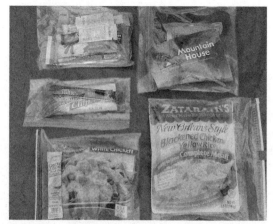

With a felt tip marker label each bag for its intended meal, that is, breakfast, morning snack, lunch, etc. There should be six bags for each day. Stow all six bags in the largest, one-gallon capacity bag and write the number of the day for which that bag is intended on the outside.

After following this procedure for each day of the trip, stow all the bags in one drawstring stuff sack. That's it—a well-organized, time and energy conserving system that will have you the envy of the other campers.

Here are a few helpful hints:

- Leave all the storage bag zippers slightly open in order to expel excess air. The bags will then lie flatter.

- A few food items may not lend themselves to apportionment, such as the ten piece pack of tortillas or the bottle of squeeze margarine. Since these, obviously, will not be consumed in one meal, pack them in their own bags then stow with the daily bags.

- Many items come in boxes and bottles that take up unnecessary space. Make the contents more compact by repackaging them into zippered bags with the box directions torn off and deposited in the bags with the food or written with marker on the outside. On the sample menu, the squeezable margarine bottle is the lone exception to this rule.

- Always carry a bottle or two of water on your bike in case of emergency or in the event there's no safe water at your campsite for drinking or cooking.

- Water that may be unsafe to drink is always unsafe to cook with, boiled or not.

Then put each day's menu selections into its own bag and mark accordingly.

- Coleman Exponent 422 multi-fuel stove or stove of your choice
- Outback Oven by Backpacker's Pantry
- MSR Base Two Pot Set – 8-inch pan
- Serving spoon and spatula

RECIPES

Baking is a hoot and your camp diet can be broadened greatly with the addition of biscuits, pies, cakes, and much more. It's also pretty easy once you get the hang of it. Of course there's a price to be paid: it takes a bit more time, a bit more foolin' around, and a whole lot more stove fuel. Here are a couple dishes I rustled up for you.

No Foolin' Pizza

If there's one thing that is guaranteed to remind you of the comforts of home, it has to be pizza. I'm not talkin' rubbery pizza from the freezer section that just gets heated up . . . no siree. I mean real, honest-to-goodness baked pizza like you get at your favorite neighborhood pizzeria. The best part of all is that you can bake it yourself, in camp, and you don't need a zillion ingredients and a degree in culinary arts, either. This is great pizza that YOU can do. I'm a kitchen klutz and I did it. Here's how:

INGREDIENTS:

- Pizza crust, 8-inch (I used Boboli brand, two per package).
- Pizza Sauce, 2.5 fl.oz. per pizza.
- Sliced Pepperoni, 1.75 oz. per pizza (approx. 25 slices)
- Grated Parmesan Cheese, approx. 2 oz. per pizza

> **WARNING: You may become the most popular camper when word gets around about your homemade pizza. And you don't even have to tell them how easy it was.**

1. Press crust into pan.

2. Add sauce, spread evenly.

3. Add Parmesan cheese.

4. Add pepperoni.

5. Light the stove and adjust heat to about medium. Place oven riser on burner and reflector collar under burner per oven instructions.

6. Cover pizza, center thermometer on lid center and place on top of riser.

7. Carefully lower oven hood onto pan. Thermometer should be visible through center hole.

8. When thermometer reaches BAKE zone, begin timing. Boboli directions call for 8 to 10 minutes at 450 degrees F. We found 10 minutes was not enough upon inspection and added another ten. Your time may vary.

9. When done baking remove fabric oven hood first and then the covered pan from stove top. Very Hot, handle with care! Remove pizza from pan with spatula and enjoy!

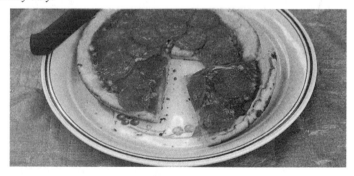

NOTES: Regulating temperature is tricky but it did not seem critical for this task. The thermometer easily went over BAKE zone but did not result in burning. Lower heat as much as you can without shutting the stove off entirely once temp reaches BURN zone. If stove does go out, don't panic; simply remove everything from stovetop and relight. Pan and lid get HOT quickly, handle with care.

Mincemeat Pie

This is my favorite pie but my wife will only bake it once a year—for Christmas dinner—as she doesn't like it. But I can bake it all I want when camping, right?

INGREDIENTS:

- 1 Package Borden None Such Classic Original Condensed Mincemeat with Apples and Raisins
- 1 box Jiffy Pie Crust Mix
- 3-4 cups water

1. Reconstitute mincemeat filling per label directions, set aside.

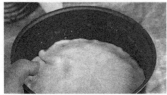

4. Spoon in cooled filling. There's not room for all of it. I ate the remainder. Lay the other dough ball in the center of a paper towel and flatten with clean hands and fingers to about 8-inch diameter. Transfer to pan and gently push the outside on to the edge of the bottom dough.

2. Empty pie crust mix into the 8-inch pan. Add water and mix with spoon until mixture is uniform. Knead with clean, bare hands. Split the dough and form two balls.

5. Cut several slits in the top to allow steam to escape. Cover with lid, thermometer, and hood and bake as with pizza. Baking time is about one hour.

3. Lay one ball of dough in the center of the pan and flatten at first with your fist and then spread evenly across bottom and up about a half-inch along sides.

7. To remove pie from pan, let cool completely then turn pan over and bring it sharply down on a flat surface covered with paper towel, foil, or paper plate. Pie will fall out in one piece. ∎

	Day 1	Day 2	Day 3	Day 4	Day 5	Day 6	Day 7
Breakfast	Tea/Coffee/ Cocoa/ Orange Juice, Apple Crisp Oatmeal, Strawberry Breakfast Bar	Tea/Cocoa/ Vanilla Coffee/ Orange Juice, Blueberry Breakfast Bar, Apricots	Tea/Hazelnut Coffee/Cocoa/ Orange Juice, Eggs & Bacon, Potato Pancakes	Tea/Coffee/ Cocoa/ Orange Juice, Maple Oatmeal, Strawberry Breakfast Bar	Tea/Cocoa/ Vanilla Coffee/ Orange Juice, Bacon, Hash Browns, Almond Breakfast Bar	Tea/Hazelnut Coffee/Cocoa/ Orange Juice, Cinnamon Oatmeal, Blueberry Breakfast Bar	Tea/Coffee/ Cocoa/ Orange Juice, Banana Bread Oatmeal, Almond Breakfast Bar
AM Snack	Grape Juice, Peanut Butter Bar	Lemon Iced Tea, Peanut Butter Crackers	Grape Juice, Almond Bar	Mandarin & Mango Green Tea, Peanut Butter Crackers	Lemon Iced Tea, Blueberry Bar	Grape Juice, Peanut Butter Crackers	Orange Juice, Trail mix
Lunch	Chicken Wraps, Cranberries & Raisins, Iced Tea	Tuna Wraps, Mixed Fruit, Coffee	Chicken Noodle Soup, Crackers, Strawberries, Grape Juice	Mac & Cheese, Cranberries & Raisins, Iced Tea	Sliced Beef Wraps, Blueberry Bar, Coffee	Chicken Wraps, Strawberry Bar, Iced Tea	Chili, Oyster Crackers, Peanut Butter Crackers, Juice
PM Snack	Raspberry Drink, Crackers with Cheddar Cheese	Iced Tea, Brownie	Orange Drink, Crackers with Cheddar Cheese	Raspberry Drink, Brownie	Grape Drink, Peanut Butter Bar	Coffee, Trail mix	Juice, Energy Bar
Dinner	Cajun Blackened Chicken with Yellow Rice	Beef Stew, Sour Cream & Chives Mashed Potatoes	Pizza, Raspberry Drink	New Orleans Style Red Beans & Rice with Sausage	Yellow Fin Tuna Fillets, Roasted Garlic Mashed Potatoes	Chicken Flavored Pasta & Sauce, Homestyle Mashed Potatoes	Pizza, Raspberry Drink
Evening Snack	Ice Cream, Cider	Mixed Fruit, Coffee	Trail mix, Cider	Ice Cream, Grape juice	Brownie, Green Tea	Ice Cream, Cider	Beef Jerky, Coffee

SAMPLE SEVEN-DAY MENU

No trip to Sturgis is complete without seeing the awesome Mt Rushmore. Photo by Jim Woofter

The Blue Ridge Parkway, a favorite ride among motorcyclists, winds 469 miles from Virginia to North Carolina through mountain meadows and past seemingly endless vistas. Photo by John Cheetham

Dealing with Beasties

You are not alone. Wherever you are, whatever you do, other creatures surround you. This is never so true as when you are camping. Fortunately, encounters with creatures at the upper end of the food chain are few and far between; indeed, the odds of being struck by lightning are far greater than meeting a bear. But it never hurts to be prepared for all the creatures, large and small, that you might meet in the great outdoors.

The creatures that campers need to be concerned about in the backcountry are those we tend to forget about in an industrialized country—microorganisms, such as protozoa, bacteria, and viruses. Many microbes are benign or even helpful to us, such as the bacteria in our own intestines that help us digest food. However, many are agents of disease that are introduced to humans by environmental vectors, insect or animal hosts. For example, most cases of infectious diarrhea and related gastrointestinal upset are caused by water-borne microorganisms.

Beware of drinking from lakes and streams. Despite their "pristine" appearances many sources of water are contaminated by bacteria and other microorganisms.

The water purifier on the left uses a plunger mechanism to bring the water in through the intake hose, while the filter on the right, shown attached to a water bottle, has a lever action. Note the float on the water hose, to keep the intake element suspended above any silt or sand.

WATER-BORNE MICROORGANISMS

Most common of the water-borne critters that cause humans problems are single-cell animals known as protozoa. *Giardia lamblia* is probably the best known in this country, though regionally, others may be more prevalent. Giardiasis, once known as "beaver fever," is spread through mammalian feces—animal and human—and for that reason it has been found in public water sources in every state in the union at one time or another as well as in the national parks and forests. Countless campers and backpackers have learned the hard way that seemingly pristine mountain lakes and streams are anything but. Concentrations of these organisms can be inversely proportional to the influx of fresh water at a particular source, so places where standing water is not replenished continuously by fresh water should be most suspect.

In addition to protozoa, there are many types of bacteria (cholera, salmonella, E. coli) and some strains of viruses (hepatitis A, polio) that can contaminate a potential water supply, though the latter hazards are currently rare in North America. The safest course is for campers to consider every water source contaminated and take steps to guard one's health from the obvious risks. This will include good general hygiene, such as washing your hands before preparing food or after visiting the latrine. Most importantly though, you will need to make your water safe by filtering out or neutralizing any contaminants. There are several ways you can accomplish this, and each has its advantages, depending on your particular circumstances.

WATER TREATMENT

The oldest method of water treatment is boiling. Water boiled for just three minutes will be sterilized of viruses, bacteria, and protozoa. Though this method can yield a large quantity of potable water, it consumes a lot of fuel and takes a fair amount of time to set up a stove, heat the water, then wait for it to cool enough to drink.

Another way to disinfect water is with a chemical additive, such as iodine, which is available for this purpose in concentrated tablets or solution. While this method is simple, convenient, and effective, you must let the water sit for approximately 20 to 30 minutes before it is safe to drink. In addition, iodine additives impart an off taste, though this can be neutralized by adding ascorbic acid (Vitamin C) or running everything through a water filter with a carbon element, which also removes organic chemicals left from pesticides and herbicides.

Instead of iodine, unscented liquid household bleach, such as Clorox, can be used. Add 2 drops per quart of water (8 drops per gallon), mix well, then let stand uncovered for 30 minutes. Store in covered container. For more information on this method see www.cpa.gov/ogwdw000/faq/emerg.html

Water filters have been the most common method of treating drinking water for many years. These mechanical gadgets pump water through a filtering element commonly made of ceramic or glass fiber that contains pores too small to let suspended contaminants pass through. The ultimate effectiveness of your filter will be determined by its pore size, measured in microns—a unit equal to one-millionth of a meter. (A human hair is approximately 100 microns thick.) Pores that are 4 microns or smaller should catch most protozoans, but to remove bacteria you will need a filter with a pore size no bigger than 0.2 microns. Viruses can be as small as 0.001 microns in size. If this is a concern, you should be shopping for a water purifier—a filter that incorporates both a mechanical filter to remove the bulk of contaminants and a second-stage iodine element to disinfect those that remain behind. To both extend the life of a filter and prevent clogging, smart campers will first pre-filter their drinking water through a coffee filter (or paper towels or a cloth like a clean bandana) before pumping it, especially when the water source is especially silty or cloudy.

~

For pure water simply dig a hole 18 inches in diameter to a depth 6 inches below the water table. After emptying this three times the water will be clear and clean.

~

Scientific innovation, in combination with military needs, has resulted in the development of a new type of water purifier that has become very popular with outdoor sportsmen who don't have easy access to clean water or can't afford the luxury of lugging along large, heavy, quantities of bottled water on their backs. Made by MSR®, the product is simply called the MIOX®. The device is 7 inches high with a 1-inch diameter and the complete kit weighs only 8 oz. The beauty of this little guy is that it doesn't filter, it actually kills everything that the filters sift out plus everything else they can't. In short, if used correctly, it produces the safest water possible. And therein is the secret. It is very hi-tech and works through a complicated, but natural, electro-chemical process, powered by batteries, utilizing only common salt. Its directions are simple but must be followed correctly. The unit works by manufacturing internally a certain quantity of water treatment compound, which you add to your water jug. After a prescribed period of time the water is safe to drink. It's that simple. One treatment with the MIOX® will produce up to 4 liters of water within 30 minutes. If the water source contains silt or sediment, pre-filter it through a coffee filter as described above to ensure the maximum effectiveness of the water treatment compound. Another small concern is that the unit's electrical power is provided by two CR123 lithium batteries. The unit does come with the batteries but users will be smart to carry spares. The good news is that because the battery is used in many cameras, it's not hard to find.

The newest in water purification systems is the MIOX® made by MSR®. Photo courtesy of Cascade Designs, Inc.

INSECTS

While not as numerous as microorganisms, insects are the creatures which you will actually see the most of while camping. Most are innocuous little guys that you hardly, if ever, are aware of, but some have the potential of being annoying, others painful, and a very rare few—deadly. Fortunately, a camper has many defenses against such things, not the least of which are the many good over-the-counter insect repellents on the market today. Although there are many "all-natural" products that can claim some effectiveness, the more toxic alternatives have been well-proven in the field.

One of the most widely used ingredients in over-the-counter insect repellants is DEET (N,N-diethyl-meta-toluamide). Developed in 1946 for use by the military in insect-infested areas, DEET is available in

Don't laugh! Flying, biting insects can really be annoying, especially during certain times of the year. Head nets and bug shirts can help save a trip. This design unzips at the neck so the wearer can flip the hood back to eat or drink.

varying strengths and is especially useful against flying and biting insects. Although it is effective, some people are quite sensitive to it. A maximum concentration of 30 percent DEET is recommended for adults, 10 percent for children under the age of twelve. Products which encapsulate the DEET in protein particles both prevent skin absorption and provide time-release benefits.

Insect repellents containing the chemical picaridin, which have been available abroad for many years, were introduced to the U.S. market in 2005. Picaridin has been found to be similar to DEET in effectiveness, but less irritating to the skin. Unlike DEET, Picaridin does not damage plastics or synthetic material.

Another chemical you will see in effective insect repellants is permethrin, which was also originally developed for military applications. An odorless repellent, permethrin should be applied to clothing and gear (not skin), where it will bond to fabric for long-lasting protection, even after repeated washings. Since permethrin is highly toxic to a wide variety of organisms including cats, fish, honey bees, and small mammals, as well as being a likely human carcinogen, you may want to think twice about using it.

ANTS

Most species of ants found in North America can bite. Of these the fire ant is the one that gets the most attention in the United States. Fortunately, these recent immigrants from South America are still restricted to the warmer southern states, but in areas where they are habituated, these small red ants can be found just about anywhere. In open areas fire ant colonies form a conical earthen mound with a hard rain-resistant crust roughly 10 to 15 inches high. They are also found in dark protected areas with sufficient moisture, such as rotten logs, building walls, under sidewalks, etc. Campers in the south are especially advised to carefully inspect potential tent sites for ant mounds or unusual concentrations of ants.

The fire ant's claim to fame derives from a propensity to be very aggressive and tenacious, gripping their prey with their jaws and delivering repeated stings with an abdominal stinger. Their tiny size belies an ability to inflict severe pain via a multi-toxin venom. If you disturb a group of them or their mound, count on all of them swarming you. Since they are sensitive to movement and vibration, your normal reaction of jerking back when you are initially stung will trigger all the others to bite, seemingly simultaneously. A normal, healthy, mobile human, who retains the ability to escape and repel attacks, is rarely in lethal danger. Victims are advised to treat these wounds as they would bee stings. There is no known repellent so you should just give fire ants a wide berth.

FLIES

While there are hundreds of varieties of flies, those that are pests to campers include horse flies, deer flies, and of course, the infamous black fly, which thrives in the cooler climates of the northernmost states and Canada. Unlike the fire ant, which stings in defense, flies bite to obtain a blood meal. The pain that we feel when bitten is not caused by the bite itself, but from an allergic reaction to the insect's saliva, which is ingeniously formulated to promote bleeding.

Black flies are about an eighth of an inch long, hatch in the spring from larvae in streams, and last until early summer. The female fly inflicts a painful, itchy bite. Many savvy visitors simply avoid traveling in these areas during fly season. If your travel plans are not so opportune, however, you do have some defense. In addition to over-the-counter insect repellents, which you may apply both to yourself and your clothing, wear long-sleeved shirts and pants with tight-fitting cuffs that will discourage the annoying little buggers from crawling inside in search of a meal. Another widely known folk repellant is

~

Always keep your tobacco pipe lit; mosquitoes will stay away.

~

Avon's Skin So Soft lotion. Among hardy outdoorsmen of all types, head nets are also popular items and they really can make a bad situation a lot more bearable.

A summer irritant is the "no-see-um," so-called because they are so small—as small as a pinhead. They can land, bite, feed, and be gone before the itch alerts you to their presence. Since no-see-ums can pass through ordinary screening, many tents have no-see-um screening with a finer mesh.

MOSQUITOES

Like flies, mosquitoes are pesky and tenacious in their search for a blood meal. The biting female, like the black fly, utilizes proteins in her saliva that prevent blood clotting and it's our allergic reaction to these venoms that cause us to itch. The habitat of the mosquito is widespread, but they breed and thrive in standing water during temperate weather. Although they are considered to be mostly a nuisance in civilized North America, mosquitoes are renowned as efficient transmitters of certain diseases, including Eastern and St. Louis encephalitis, West Nile virus, dengue fever, yellow fever, malaria, and many other ailments typically associated with the tropics. Fortunately, mosquitoes are very sensitive to insect repellents, so you can minimize any risks with a little prevention.

BEES AND WASPS

To most people bees and wasps are more of a nuisance than a deadly threat. Their vegetarian diet, the location of their venom mechanisms, and the type of toxin in their venom are all evidence that sting-

Bees and wasps only sting in defense, though they can easily misinterpret our usual reaction to them as a threat.

ing is a defensive act in reaction to a perceived threat—they don't use their toxin to obtain food. So there's a lot of truth in the adage that if you let them alone, they'll leave you alone. Unfortunately, bright-colored clothing, the scent of shampoo and other toiletries, as well as the sugary smell of soft drinks and other food odors confuse and attract them, and your sudden negative reaction to the appearance of a bee can easily be perceived as threatening enough to trigger a stinging defense. The good news is that the toxin in their venom is designed to send an immediate and sharp message of warning to the recipient rather than generate a long-lasting or permanent effect. When human fatalities do occur (around 25 each year throughout the United States) the victims were generally found to be unusually allergic to the venom. People with known allergies to bee and wasp toxin should carry an emergency sting kit when outdoors and should inform their traveling companions of their condition and what they can do in an emergency, if necessary.

TICKS

Although the idea of finding a tick attached to your body is repulsive, the problem with ticks is not their bite, but the diseases they might transmit to you in the process. Worldwide, only mosquitoes transmit more diseases than ticks. Ticks do not jump or fly, but instead live in wooded brush and long grass and rely on making direct contact with an animal host and crawling aboard. From there, they usually mi-

Many of the ticks that carry disease seek out deer and mice as hosts. Controlling deer populations is quite a concern in some areas of the country, as natural predators are forced out of the picture by ongoing development.

grate to the warmest spot they can find on a body; this might be along the hairline at the nape of your neck, or it might involve a more . . . intimate location. Regular application of an insect repellent such as DEET, wearing long-sleeved shirts, and pants tucked into the tops of your boots should thwart them; light-colored clothing will make them easier to spot. To properly remove an attached tick, grasp it with a pair of thin-nosed precision tweezers right at the level of your skin and pull firmly and steadily backward without jerking, twisting, or squeezing its body. The object is to remove the whole tick. Its head is very small and if broken off would remain in the skin and could cause an infection.

There are two basic types of ticks one should be keeping an eye out for. The deer tick is only as large as a poppy seed when young and a sesame seed when mature, yet it is credited with spreading Lyme disease, named for the Connecticut town that was associated with an outbreak in 1975. Although the heaviest concentration of Lyme-infected deer, mice, and ticks occur throughout the New England states, their populations are increasing in the mid-Atlantic states as well.

The second type of tick is commonly referred to as a dog tick or wood tick and is about the circumference of a pencil eraser before it becomes distended with a blood meal. It has been credited with the transmission of several strains of disease, the most prevalent of which is Rocky Mountain Spotted Fever, which can be fatal. RMSF has been diagnosed in every U.S. state except Maine, Alaska, and Hawaii; despite its name, most cases occur in the southeastern United States. Since ticks must be attached to an animal 36 to 48 hours before the disease pathogens transfer into a new host, preventative measures and careful, daily self-inspections should keep you healthy.

SPIDERS

People are generally fearful of spiders because of centuries of negative fiction that revolve around a very few species. The truth is that these animals are shy creatures when it comes to humans, or for that matter, any animal too large to eat. Their hollow fangs and venom are specifically designed for capturing, immobilizing, and killing insects for food, not for preying on people. Of the approximately 177,000 species of spiders found around the world, the only two that

~

Cover your motorcycle seat while in camp with a piece of oil cloth tightly tied in place; otherwise mice and other critters may eat the leather during the night.

~

The web of a black widow spider is typically disorganized, not the neat concentric structure we usually associate with spider webs.

pose any risk at all to campers in the United States are the black widow and the brown recluse, and their bites are rarely fatal to humans. Before black widow antivenom was developed, only five percent of people bitten died, and now fewer than six deaths a year can be directly attributed to bites. The fatality rate for recluse bites is even smaller.

Both species of spiders are nocturnal, preferring to hide during the day in wood piles and under logs and rocks. Outbuildings such as sheds and privies are favorite indoor locales where both species can find an abundant supply of food in the form of other insects. The adult female black widow spider is approximately 1 1/2 inches long, from foot to foot, and she sports a distinctive red hourglass design on the underside of her abdomen. A black widow's web is characteristically disorganized, not the photogenic concentric forms we typically picture. In contrast, recluse spiders rely on hunting skills rather than webs to obtain their food. While both spiders use their venom to kill or immobilize their prey, bites to humans generally occur only when the spiders become trapped between one's body and something else, such as when you sit on or grasp a log where the spider is resting.

When initially bitten by one of these spiders, one may feel little more than a pinprick, if that. Victims may not be aware that they have been bitten until symptoms start to occur ten minutes to hours afterward. A black widow bite may cause painful abdominal muscle cramping, nausea, and difficulty breathing. Recluse bites typically progress from nausea and localized itching to a painful and debilitating ulceration of the skin around the bite site. While the very young and old are at most risk, all victims are advised to seek medical assistance as soon as practical. Antivenoms are available and are most ef-

Scorpion stings can be painful, but they are usually not deadly.

fective when administered as soon after the bite as possible. First aid includes cold packs applied to the bite site along with aspirin or ibuprofen to ease muscle cramping.

The black widow makes its home along the eastern seaboard from Massachusetts to Florida and across the southern tier states. Although the brown recluse spider has been found as far north as Ohio, their normal range covers an area from Texas across the southern states to the Carolinas and northward from the Gulf of Mexico to the Ohio River.

SCORPIONS

A number of species of scorpions are native to the United States, but the stings of all but one, found in Arizona, western New Mexico, and southeastern California, are no more harmful than a bee sting.

Scorpions have much in common with the black widow and the recluse spiders, including their dislike of daylight, fondness for dark, damp, daytime hiding places; and their preference for nocturnal hunting. They also share their reluctance for human contact and resort to stinging only as a defensive tool. Like most defensive assaults, this one produces sharp, intense pain. If the sting originates from a dangerous scorpion, other symptoms may quickly follow: nausea, vomiting, and possibly respiratory and/or cardiac distress. Again, those at the highest risk are the very young and old. First aid includes applying ice and transporting the victim to medical care. Antivenoms are commonly available at medical facilities in scorpion territory and are very effective.

When camping in scorpion territory, it's a good idea to examine bedding before retiring and to shake out shoes, boots, and clothing prior to dressing in the morning. Be particularly careful when picking up objects that have lain on the floor or ground overnight, as scorpions love to hide underneath such things.

~

Turn your boots over before putting them on in case there's a scorpion inside.

~

225

~

Snakes rarely crawl into tents.

~

SNAKES

One of the most disgusting displays of camper ignorance that I ever witnessed occurred one summer afternoon in a rural Ohio campground several years ago. Women and children from several campsites were screaming and running about while others pointed to an object on the ground—apparently the cause of their horror. It was a snake, curled up and too afraid to move. Before I could intervene, a half-dozen men proceeded to violently beat the snake with logs and stones. The snake, of course, was reduced to a bloody, broken corpse, while the men boasted of their heroic deed. Little did they realize, or even care, that what they had just unashamedly murdered was a harmless black rat snake.

Of the 127 species of snakes native to the United States, only four are poisonous: the rattlesnake, cottonmouth (water moccasin), coral snake, and copperhead. The rest, including the rat snake that met its demise in the campground, are non-poisonous and quite beneficial to people, consuming rodents like the ones responsible for the spread of the tick-borne diseases covered earlier and the deadly Hantavirus in the American Southwest. Snakes prefer to live where they can keep warm, consequently there are more species located in the south than in the north. Only 23 species of snakes are found in Canada and none at all in Alaska.

Despite the fact that only four native species are poisonous, most snakes will bite as a defensive maneuver. Since snakes typically lie in wait for their prey (as opposed to seeking it out) their favorite haunts can be found along trails, beside logs, under the overhangs of rocks and boulders, and other concealed spots within striking distance of potential prey. Experienced hikers and campers take the time to look at where they plan to place their hands and feet.

There are many myths surrounding first aid for snakebites that have been reinforced in vintage movies and cowboy novels; most of these old practices will actually do more harm than good. For example, tourniquets should be avoided, as the restriction in circulation can cause lasting tissue damage, as can incising the bite wounds to "suck" the poison out by mouth. Snake venom is almost instantly absorbed and begins dispersing throughout the body via either the lymphatic or blood circulatory systems; there is no unabsorbed pool of venom waiting to be either extracted or absorbed by the body. There is also no benefit from applying ice to the bite wound, which can permanently damage unaffected tissue.

First aid treatment for a poisonous snakebite should include removing rings, watches, and other restrictive jewelry or clothing in anticipation of broad swelling. If ice is available, it should be applied, not to the wound, but to the victim's forehead, as keeping the victim as calm as possible slows the dispersion of venom. To further retard systemic dissemination of the venom, the limb should be immobilized and the victim transported to medical care as soon as possible.

~

Do not kill snakes that are not poisonous.

~

SKUNKS AND RACCOONS

Far from shrinking in numbers as a result of suburban sprawl, skunks and raccoons have adapted quite well to human pressure and thrive in record numbers. They have become so accustomed to the presence of humans that they're now a common presence in campgrounds—especially nocturnally—as they scavenge for leftover,

Raccoons and skunks have become well adapted to scavenging from humans. Keep your camp neat and store and dispose of food properly.

227

discarded, or improperly stored food. A more serious twist to this problem has become the proliferation of rabies within their populations and the correspondent risk of human infection. Campers are cautioned to keep their camps neat and store food properly to avoid encounters with all skunks and raccoons. You should report any you see acting aggressive, sick, or disoriented.

BEARS

Even before the weather turns warm enough in the spring to get the bike out and your gear together, there will be 330,000 U.S. and another 370,000 Canadian outdoor denizens already roaming the most popular camping destinations. Who are they? Retirees? Gold Wingers? No, they're black bears! While at one time black bears could be found in every state, they still call forty states and all Canadian provinces, except Prince Edward Island, home. In the United States, their populations are concentrated throughout all of the New England states, the Allegheny, Smokey, and Ozark Mountains areas, the entire length of the Rocky Mountain chain, northern California, Oregon, and Washington, and upper regions of Minnesota, Wisconsin, and Michigan.

Brown bears, or grizzly bears as they are sometimes known, number less than 400 in the lower 48 states. These are concentrated in the greater Yellowstone area, the Bitterroot Range of the northern Rocky Mountains, the Cascade Mountain range of northern Washington, and the San Juan Mountains of southern Colorado.

With this many bears living in what are arguably the most popular camping areas in the world, is it any wonder, once tourist season gets into full swing, that bear encounters occur? One thing you can be sure of, if you're serious about motorcycle camping, sooner or later you'll find yourself in bear territory.

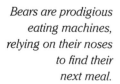

Bears are prodigious eating machines, relying on their noses to find their next meal.

Woe to the person who stands between a bear and his appetite!

THE NATURE OF THE BEAST

First and foremost, bears are prodigious eating machines. This is what they do best and most often, locating their food with a sense of smell that is absolutely awesome. They can smell soda pop through an unopened can, they can smell yesterday's food on your clothes, an unopened candy bar in your backpack or tent, leftover fries in a locked car, and vanilla-scented shampoo in your hair. Unfortunately, they don't discriminate between actual food and things that merely smell tasty. If their nose approves of something, they will try to eat it, and their bodies will simply pass anything that is indigestible. They will break into locked cars and camp coolers, rip open backpacks, and tear into occupied and unoccupied tents after anything they think is food. Rangers have reported that motorcycle saddlebags closely resemble coolers and are not uncommon targets for hungry bruins. Woe to the mere human who thinks he can stand between a bear and his appetite.

To keep your camp safe in bear country, never store food, scented toiletries, cosmetics (they contain animal fat), or toothpaste in your tent. Packs that have previously held food should also not be kept in your tent, even if they are now empty. Hang all tempting supplies in sealed containers out of reach; bears will seek out easier pickings. Picnic tables and other surfaces should be kept clean of all food residues and you should not burn table scraps or food wrappers in your fire, as the scent can travel for miles.

Do not dispense bear spray on yourself or around your camp as a method of deterring bears. Tests have shown that the scent, over long distances, actually attracts bears. Most importantly, don't feed the bears. It's dangerous, illegal, and if you're lucky enough to get away with it, encourages bruins to become camp bears that eventually must be relocated or destroyed.

CLOSE ENCOUNTERS

Notwithstanding television shows and feature movies that portray bears, especially blacks, as playful creatures cavorting for cameras in exchange for handouts or a pat on the head, campers must never forget that bears are dangerous, unpredictable wild creatures. And although human-bear encounters are frequently accidental, all are potentially disastrous.

Bears always have the upper hand in the outdoors. So acute is a bear's sense of smell that they can usually detect your presence in the woods well before either of you can see or hear each other. In most cases bears will go the other way before you even know they're around; they wish to avoid you as much as you should wish to avoid them. Experienced outdoorsmen whistle, sing, or talk loudly to themselves as a way of alerting bears they're in the area. You should also try to be aware of the sort of things that attract bears and avoid their food sources, like ripe berry patches or animal carcasses.

If, despite all your precautions, a meeting does occur, in most cases the bear will turn tail and flee. If your encounter is an exception, try to remain calm. First, look for cubs. If there are any and they run away, the encounter will likely end at this point. If no cubs are present, you can encourage a happy ending by not turning and running away. Even if the bear has no untoward intentions, your fleeing will be an invitation to chase you down. Similarly, try not to show weakness and fear, but avoid eye contact which can be threatening. Talk quietly and calmly to the bear while backing slowly away. Throwing away your backpack or coat as a diversion is rarely effective; instead, leave them on to protect your back and neck from more serious injury. Attempting to climb trees is rarely successful. To begin with, you must out-pace an animal that can sprint 45 mph, you must choose a tree that can support both your combined weights, and you must climb faster and higher than the bear.

Wear your sidearm and bowie knife at all times when not sleeping. It's a good idea, too, to keep a camp rifle loaded and handy.

Your next line of defense depends on the type of bear you're confronted with. Oddly enough, although brown bears are several times the size of black bears, your chances of survival may actually be better if you are attacked by one. Most often a brown bear's motive for attacking is to neutralize, but not kill, a perceived threat. They frequently feel satisfied after cuffing or mauling a victim, and afterwards may leave the scene. Victims who curl up in a ball while protecting the back of their necks with their hands and playing dead are usually left alive.

Black bear attacks are a different story. They will surely attack for the same defensive reasons as described above but, unlike brown bears, blacks will stalk and kill a human for food. Consequently, when black bears attack, their primary goal is almost always to kill. Never play dead when attacked by a black bear. You should fight back as if your life were at stake.

All in all, your best defense in the face of an attack is bear (pepper) spray. Pepper spray is credited with saving so many lives that it is issued as standard equipment in Alaska to outdoor workers, including loggers, rangers, surveyors, and utility crews. But to be of any use it must be conveniently at hand when you need it; make sure to carry it in a holster on your belt and not in your backpack.

~

Extra cartridges should be stored wrapped in oilcloth to prevent the brass from tarnishing.

~

When traveling in bear country, whistle or talk loudly to alert any bears in the vicinity of your presence. Most likely they will want to avoid you as much as you want to avoid them. Photo courtesy of Mike Bender, USFWS.

231

"Leaves of three, let it be."

POISON IVY

Poison ivy or one of its Rhus genus cousins—poison oak and poison sumac—can be found throughout North America, with the exception of Alaska, Hawaii, and Nevada. These plants are a serious concern for campers, as contact with any part of them results in an allergic reaction that may range from mildly irritating to completely debilitating, due to an oil called urushiol (oo-ROO-shee-ol), which is found on the plants' leaves, stems, and roots. Since there is a delay of anywhere from a day to a week before the onset of the first symptoms, washing exposed skin promptly has long been used in an attempt to prevent or mitigate the resulting skin irritation. However, some authorities now believe water actually helps to spread the oil, thus broadening the area of infection. Accordingly, some have found that first rinsing the area with something that dissolves oil, such as fingernail polish remover, gasoline, or turpentine, has lessened and even prevented the rash, if done immediately. The bottom line is that nothing is guaranteed to work and campers are advised to use due caution.

Urushiol is a tenacious oil that knows no seasons, expiration dates, or boundaries. It is equally hazardous in winter as summer and it does not evaporate, dry up, or become less potent as it ages. Any object—pets, clothing, boots, firewood, tools—that has touched the plant will transport the oil and should be washed or discarded to avoid infecting another. Likewise, the smoke from burning poison ivy plants or wood that has been exposed to the oil can produce life-threatening internal complications. Contact with the blisters of the rash itself or the liquid they contain will not spread the outbreak, nor will scratching cause the rash to spread, though it could cause infection or scarring. An apparent spreading of the rash after the initial breakout is due to a delayed absorption of oil or re-exposure to contaminated clothing, tools, or pets.

A typical poison ivy rash may last about two weeks and minor cases often are left untreated. In that time, the body will have succeeded in destroying the contaminated cells, while hormones known as corticosteroids will have reduced inflammation. Various topical treatments available over the counter may be used to reduce itching of small rashes, but medical intervention in the form of additional corticosteroids (prednisone) may be required in some cases.

Of the three plants, poison ivy and oak are the most widespread and, fortunately, the easiest to identify. Their leaves resemble the shape of an elongated playing-card spade with jagged or toothed edges. The tips of poison ivy leaves are pointed, while those of poison oak are slightly blunted. On both plants, the leaves grow in groups of three at the ends of each stalk, two of which will have short stems of equal length oriented in a V-shape with a third, noticeably longer stem, extending from its apex. The leaves will be a glossy dark green during the summer, reddish in the spring, and a combination of red, orange, bronze, and darker green in the fall. Poison ivy and oak may grow either as a ground-based plant or as a climbing vine. Geographically, poison ivy is more concentrated in the eastern half of the United States, while poison oak appears most often throughout the west coast, the south, and the eastern seaboard.

Human encounters with poison sumac are rarer, since this plant's preferred habitat is where people generally don't go—perennially wet areas such as swamps and sloughs. Sumac's appearance is also different from poison ivy and oak; it grows as a tall shrub or small tree and resembles its harmless cousin, the staghorn sumac, which is frequently seen growing in highway drainage areas in the east. Six to twelve long, narrow, dark green leaves will be arranged opposite one another along a single stem, with a final, single leaf at the tip. Finally, where the staghorn sumac is noted by its unique, erect, horn-shaped clusters of dark orange berries, those of poison sumac are whitish-green and drooping.

~

Wads of green leaves serve well as toilet paper. It's advised not to use poison ivy leaves.

~

His and hers by Lake Ontario.

You meet the nicest people, er, moose on a Honda.
Photo by Linda Knepp

After the Trip

Been there, done that. The first thing every rider wants to do after a long trip is shut off the bike, strip off their riding gear and flop on the couch. Don't do it. Remember the old movie westerns where the cowpokes looked to the welfare of their horses before themselves? Well, your expensive camping gear is the equivalent of those horses. As soon as you dismount, unpack your tent and sleeping bag and see to them. If you don't, like an exhausted horse, they may suffer irreparable harm. If you take care of them right away, they will pay you back by lasting a whole lot longer.

Your first chore is to string up a sturdy bit of clothesline . . . or two. Some campers have found that two parallel lines, about two feet apart, more or less, along with a line prop-pole, have the strength necessary to support a tent. Next, open all the zippers on doors, screens, and windows. Now, turn the tent inside out and spread open as far as possible on the clotheslines. If you live where this is not possible, set up the tent in your house or apartment. If even this isn't possible drape the tent over a table, couch, or your bed and turn it like a piece of roasting meat every 30 minutes for at least four hours. The purpose of this exercise is to rid the tent of as much dampness as possible, and to circulate clean air to every nook and cranny.

With soft goods like tents and sleeping bags, the primary concern on returning home is to prevent the growth of mildew, a very common fungus that thrives on cloth and leather, especially in moist,

As soon as you arrive home, hang out your tent and fly to dry thoroughly before storage. Photo by Tara Hartman

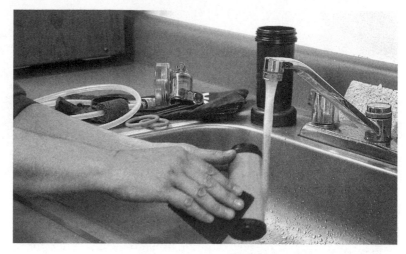

Once you are back home, some water filters can be scrubbed clean to give them a longer life in the field.

dark environments. And don't assume that your gear is okay because it never got wet. That's a misconception that can come back to haunt you. Microscopic mildew spores are constantly around us. They occur naturally in the environment—on grasses, weeds, and simply wafting through the air. When a spore (and all it takes is one) alights on something it recognizes as food, like fabric, it germinates and expands to resemble a grayish-white snowflake, eventually maturing to release more spores. Mildew colonies not only can leave an item stained and smelling musty, they physically degrade the material itself. In addition, mildew can actually thrive between the fabric and the waterproof coating of your tent, eventually causing the urethane to delaminate and flake away.

Although you cannot reverse any damage done by mildew, you can stop the problem from getting any worse if you catch it early. At your first opportunity, unpack your tent, open all the zippers and flaps, and give it a good chance to dry out thoroughly, in the sunlight if possible. Just remember that too much sun exposes the fabric to ultraviolet light, which is also harmful. If you cannot pitch your tent outside, you could hang it up in your garage. Lightly brush away any surface grime and give any attention to stains that could benefit from a spot cleaning.

If your tent is really dirty or mildewed, you will need to give it a good hand wash with lukewarm water and a mild detergent, such as Cold Water Woollite. If you can, erect the tent and use a sponge to clean every surface and corner, inside and out; don't forget the bottom! Rinse everything well before air-drying thoroughly. Manufacturers warn against the use of clothes dryers as this can damage waterproof coatings.

Tackle any evidence of mildew with a mixture of one cup of Lysol in a bucket of warm water. While you are at it, don't forget to give your lowly ground cloth a good going over, so it won't be harboring any mildew spores which can transfer to your nice clean tent. Before packing things away at the end of a season, take care of any routine repairs or maintenance chores, such as resealing seams or revitalizing the water-repellant coating on your rain fly. For long-term storage, don't return your tent to its stuff sack; instead, pack it loosely in a large box or drawstring bag that will allow for the circulation of air.

SLEEPING GEAR

A good sleeping bag is a marvelous thing and one worth taking care of. When you get home, hang it up to dry and air out. If you make an effort to keep your bag reasonably clean, you can avoid washing it more often than is otherwise necessary, since laundering can be a pretty traumatic process for both the insulation and construction. When body oils accumulate in the lining, however, the material will no longer be able to function at its best. Sleeping bags can be hand washed in a bathtub, but a front-loading washing machine is preferred; never use a top-loading machine as the agitation can cause permanent damage. Use cold water and non-detergent soap; there are also many special wash-in treatments for down insulation on the market today. After a thorough rinse, drain as much water as you can from the wet bag and handle it so as not to strain seams and baffles. Either hang to dry, supporting it well along its length, or use a large commercial dryer set on low heat. A couple tennis balls thrown into the dryer with the bag may help break up any clumps of insulation.

Like tents, sleeping bags should be stored loosely (an old pillow case works great), not only to benefit from the free circulation of air, but also to prevent the insulating materials from developing a "memory" of their compressed state that would thereafter prevent them from expanding to their full loft. Cots and sleeping pads typically only need spot cleaning but everything should be put away dry, of course. Store a self-inflating mattress unrolled with the valve open, so it can expand fully and benefit from circulating air.

~

Camp cooking needn't be fancy but it must be satisfying.

~

KITCHEN STUFF

Stoves and water filters may represent some of the more mechanical items in a camper's arsenal, but they are usually pretty simple units overall, with parts that can be serviced easily in the field. "Servicing" usually means cleaning, however, and that is a job that can almost always be done most thoroughly at home, where you have plenty of good, hot water at hand. Give all cookware a nice scrubbing with soap and dry thoroughly. Launder any sacks that held food items, and rotate any remaining edible staples back into your pantry at home. Stoves can take a lot of abuse in a pack and lightweight parts can get bent out of alignment. O-ring seals and pump washers should be checked and lubricated periodically to ensure safe, efficient operation. Carbon deposits will wipe off easily with a scrubbing pad.

Most general stove maintenance involves liquid-fuel burners, as they do not operate as cleanly as those that use pressurized gas canisters. Liquid fuel that is ignited before it has been pressurized into a vapor, as when you are priming your stove, will burn with a yellow flame and produce soot; once it has passed through the vaporizing jet, it burns clean and blue. When you turn off your fuel supply to your stove, it's a good practice to blow out the pilot before the flame turns messy. The remaining raw fuel in the pressurized line will help to keep the jet and the line cleaner. Many manufacturers supply small maintenance kits for their stoves and you should follow their recommendations. Never store liquid fuel in the stove between trips, as debris, condensation, and gasoline additives can really gum up all the works over time. Rinse empty fuel tanks with clean fuel and cap them loosely.

All water filters can be prone to clogging, especially when the water you must treat has a lot of suspended sediment. To stretch the life of your filter element in the field, let cloudy water settle out before pumping, or use a pre-filter. If you can clean your filter, follow your manufacturer's instructions, and wash your hands before and after with clean water. When reassembling everything, check all O-rings and seals to make sure they are pliable and in good repair. Once you have taken a filter apart for cleaning, many people recommend flushing the unit with a weak solution of two teaspoons of household bleach in one quart of water, to discourage the growth of any lingering microorganisms during storage.

~

Take along a small bottle of powdered alum in your first-aid kit; its good for mouth sores.

~

WATERPROOF-BREATHABLE FABRICS

Gore-Tex and similar waterproof-breathable laminates benefit greatly from periodic maintenance to keep them functioning at their best. Spot clean any stains before washing with a powdered non-detergent soap or proprietary treatment for such materials. As with any waterproof garment, they're only as good as the DWR (Durable Water Repellency) on the outer fabric. Over time, these treatments will lose effectiveness, allowing water to saturate the outer fabric, so even if it can't leak through the inner membrane, you will feel damp and clammy as if it were. To revitalize the factory DWR, machine dry your gear with medium heat or iron it carefully with a warm iron (really!). If you need to enhance the DWR performance of an older piece, use either a fluoropolymer spray, such as 3M Scotchguard, or a wash-in treatment, like Nikwax's TX-Direct.

A GEAR STORAGE SYSTEM

There are a lot of bits and pieces that comprise camping gear and it's incredibly easy for them to get scattered all over the place. You won't realize how important a storage system is until after a period of time you need to find something . . . and can't. It can be really frustrating to be forced to buy something you know you already have. However, all the problems caused by disorganization can be headed off with a storage system.

Tote boxes of uniform sizes are a good start at keeping gear organized.

Before venturing out on your first big trip, buy enough plastic tubs of the same size to store everything on your return. Large tubs with tight fitting lids are best. If they have ventilation slots or holes, use heavy duct tape to seal these shut. You won't need any insects or spiders finding their way into your gear during storage. Remember that your tent will need a tub for itself as well as each sleeping bag. On your return and after completing all the steps and procedures explained above, begin packing the gear into the tubs. Record on a separate sheet of paper for each tub every item going into that tub. When the tub is full, tape the sheet to the outside of the tub where you will be able to read it. Store the tent and its fly loosely on top of its poles, stakes, and any guy lines in one tub. Before tightly closing the lid insert at least one 3 by 6 inch bag of desiccant. See resource list for source. Store each sleeping bag—loose not rolled—in its own tub with a desiccant bag as well.

(Desiccant bags are those tiny little white bags that are usually packed with electronic or camera equipment. They are designed to absorb moisture that results in mildew and tarnish.)

Tents and sleeping bags are stored as loose as possible in their own individual totes. One or two bags of desiccant go into each tote to absorb moisture.

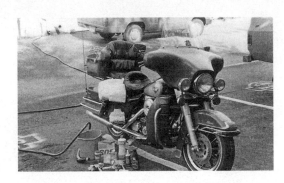

A good wash area will have protection from the sun, good drainage, and a nearby water supply. Photo by David Jacobs

MOTORCYCLE CARE

Seeing how your trusty steed got you there and back, it deserves some TLC too. Remove the luggage from your bike and wash off all those miles of accumulated dirt and road grime. Then get out the special cleaners and go after all the tar specks, bug splat, and brake pad dust. And as long as you've come that far, why not go for the wax and polish? A thorough detailing will give you a chance to inspect everything closely; on a long trip it's not unusual for parts to leak, loosen, fracture, or go missing altogether.

Once your bike's exterior has been cared for, it will be time to turn your attention inward. With the assistance of your owner's manual, check all fluid levels and perform any routine maintenance and adjustments that are due: change the oil and filter, check and top off coolant, brake fluid, and battery water. Inspect brake pads and spin both tires looking for cuts and imbedded objects, such as nails and screws. Finally, hook up the battery tender to restore a full charge.

SHARING AND SAVING YOUR ADVENTURE

Who doesn't get a kick out of relating tales and showing pictures of their trips? Probably no one. And there's no better time to get everything organized than as soon as you're back home while everything you did, everything you saw and experienced is still fresh in your mind.

If you have film that needs to be processed or images to be printed, drop them off. While you're waiting to get the pictures back pick out an album to display them. Now, everybody knows that scrapbooking has become very popular, but it's not just for wedding and baby memories. And (for you guys) it's not just a girl thing, either. Think of a scrapbook simply as a large album that has room for other stuff too,

~

To make a dinner fork, split the end of a green stick in several places.

~

Call it a scrapbook or an enhanced photo album. In either case it will help preserve the memories of your trip.

like unique bottle labels, cocktail napkins, postcards, matchbook covers, copies of traffic tickets, you know, good stuff. And guys, if you can't find a scrapbook cover that's masculine enough, make one out of wood as I did and decorate it as you wish. You could route out a space in the cover to insert a favorite photo, for example, and then cut letters with your fret saw to glue on. How about a cover made of diamond plate aluminum? The possibilities are endless.

The key to a great scrapbook is all the other items that accompany the images like promotional brochures, menus, admission ticket stubs, postcards, receipts, and so forth. What traveler doesn't come home with handfuls of stuff he didn't have when he started out? This is all fodder for the scrapbook. Just as important as this material is your own personal narrative. Now you don't have to be a professional writer to do this, but just a simple line or two describing what is pictured in each image, or a paragraph describing each leg of the journey is all that's required. By the way, make sure the book illustrates your trip in chronological order from the first day of the trip to the last.

Scrapbooking guarantees that your memories will be around for everyone to see, understand, and appreciate for many decades to come. It sure beats a shoebox of pictures.

BLOGS AND YOU

Among the many historical sites to be seen in London, England is the corner of Hyde Park closest to Marble Arch. At first glance the corner appears to be like any other park corner in the world, merely the convergence of two streets and sidewalks. On any day, that is, except Sundays. On Sundays this innocuous bit of urban real estate becomes the world famous Speakers Corner; the place where anyone can come, throw down an empty wooden soap box to stand on, and speak on any topic he chooses to anyone who will listen. It's been a London tradition since around 1872.

One hundred thirty years later Internet blogs are everyman's Speaker's Corner. As long as a person owns or at least has access to a computer that is connected to the Internet he can have his own corner on the world, a blog. A blog (short for "web log") is a permanent site on the Internet where the owner (the blogger) can post anything he wants that is legal. Blogs are worthy of your attention after your trip because it's a fantastic place for you to share your biking adventure with others. Think of it as a scrapbook that is shared, not with just a few friends and relatives, but with the world. On your blog you may post your photos, written comments and descriptions—even the ticket stubs and speeding tickets you treasure most.

And the best part is, it's free, and the second best part is, it's easy: no rocket-science degree required.

To learn how to set up a blog go to one of the many web hosts that support them. You can find oodles of these by using a search engine such as Google or Yahoo to search for "creating a blog from scratch." After a little experimenting I discovered that while there are many blog hosting sites, some are more user friendly than others. A couple things to look for when choosing your own host are the presence of templates, and prominent and easy to follow directions for adding and editing text and image content. The site that I finally went with is wordpress.com and my blog is at kuulbeemer.wordpress.com and the name of my blog is (what else?) Bob Woofter's Motorcycle Camping.

~

No one should plan on camping more than a day or two without the tools and ability to make their own furniture.

~

Equipment Suppliers

CAMPING GEAR

Cabela's
1 Cabela Drive
Sidney, Nebraska 69160
800-237-4444
www.cabelas.com

Manufacturers and retailers of a huge variety of camping and hunting gear, as well as outdoor clothing

Campmor
28 Parkway - Box 700
Saddle River, New Jersey 07458
800-226-7667
www.campmor.com

Well-established mail order supplier of outdoor gear including backpacking, climbing, and canoeing equipment and clothing

The Coleman Co.
P.O. Box 2931
Wichita, Kansas 67201
800-835-3278
www.coleman.com

One of the original manufacturers of camping equipment still offering a complete range of outdoor gear

Eureka
625 Conklin Road
Binghamton, New York 13903
888-6-EUREKA
www.eurekacamping.com

A major manufacturer of tents

Expedition Equipment
US Source: Outdoor Research
2203 1st Ave South
Seattle, Washington 98134
888-467-4327
www.outdoorresearch.com

Manufacturers of fine tents, mats, sleeping bags, etc.

Kelty Pack, Inc.
6235 Lookout Road
Boulder, Colorado 80301
800-423-2320
www.kelty.com

High quality tents and packs

Kermit Chair Company
5233 Pine Hill Road
Nashville, Tennessee 37221
888-729-9836
www.kermitchair.com

The must-have chair for motorcycle campers, available directly from manufacturer via phone or at selected rallies

Mountain Hardware
4911 Central Avenue
Richmond, California 94804
800-953-8375
www.mountainhardware.com

Manufacturers of good-quality tents, sleeping bags, clothing, and other camping gear

MSR (Mountain Safety Research)
P.O. Box 24547
Seattle, Washington 98124
800-531-9531
www.msrcorp.com

Climbing gear, stoves, cookware, water filters, and more

The North Face, Inc.
2013 Farallon Drive
San Leandro, California 94577
www.thenorthface.com

High-quality four-season/extreme-use tents and sleeping bags

Primus AB
Box 1366
171-26 Solna, Sweden
www.primus.se

Manufacturer of high-quality, compact stoves

Sierra Designs

1255 Powell Street
Emeryville, California 94608
800-635-0461
www.sierradesigns.com

Manufacturer of high-quality outdoor gear

MOTORCYCLE LUGGAGE, GEAR, AND CLOTHING

Auburn Leather

P.O. Box 338
Auburn, Kentucky 42206-0338
800-635-0617
www.auburnleather.com

Leather saddlebags and accessories

Champion Sidecars

7442 Mountjoy Drive
Huntington Beach, California 92648
800-875-0949; 714-847-1539
www.championsidecars.com

Sidecars, cargo trailers, hard saddlebags, and hard tail trunks

Chase Harper

P.O. Box 4098
Santa Barbara, California 93101
877-965-7977
www.chaseharper.com

Soft luggage supplier

Eclipse, Inc.

8901 Whittaker Road
Ypsilante, Michigan 48197
800-666-1500; 734-971-5552
www.eclipseluggage.com

Tailbags, saddlebags, tankbags. USA made

Firstgear/Tucker Rocky

4900 Alliance Gateway Freeway
Fort Worth, Texas 76177
866-302-5676; 817-258-9008
www.firstgear-usa.com

Manufacturers of a variety of gear, including soft luggage and clothing

GIVI U.S.A, Inc.

805 Pressley Road #101
Charlotte, North Carolina 28217
704-679-4123; 877-679-GIVI
www.giviusa.com

Manufacturer of motorcycle luggage

Happy Trails Motorcycle Products

4545 W. Chinden Blvd.
Boise, Idaho, 83714
800-444-8770
www.happy-trail.com

Manufacturers of aluminum saddlebags

Jesse Luggage Systems

7591 N. 74th Avenue - Suite 102
Glendale, Arizona 85303
623-878-7113
www.jesseluggage.com

Manufacturers of aluminum saddlebags

Joe Rocket

Outer Space Sports
5100 Ure Street
Tecumseh, Ontario, Canada N0R 1L0
800-635-6103
www.joerocket.com

Manufacturer of soft luggage and clothing

Kathy's Bags

Bob's BMW
10720 Guilford Road
Jessup, Maryland 20794
800-269-2627; 800-BMW-BOBS
www.bobsbmw.com

Soft luggage liners

LeatherLyke

P.O. Box 41
Bulverde, Texas 78163
800-594-2008
www.leatherlyke.com

Leather-like covered hard saddlebags

Marsee Design

Racer Parts Wholesale
411 Dorman
Indianapolis, Indiana 46202
800-397-7815; 317-639-0725
www.marseeproducts.com

Soft luggage manufacturer

Nelson-Rigg USA

3518-A Lake Center Drive
Santa Ana, California 92704
714-850-1811
www.nelsonrigg.com

Soft luggage

Rev-Pack

Box 175
New Cuyama, California 93254
800-766-2461
www.revpack.com

Soft luggage manufacturer

Roadgear, Inc.

206 West Elgin Drive
Pueblo West, Colorado
800-854-4327
www.roadgear.com

Variety of soft luggage, clothing, and motorcycle equipment

RKA

1423A Grove Street
Healdsburg, California 95448
800-349-1-RKA; 707-579-5045
www.rka-luggage.com

Soft luggage. USA made

SargentCycle Products

44 East First Street
Jacksonville, Florida 32206
800-749-7328; 800-749-SEAT
www.sargentcycle.com

Tankbag and motorcycle seat manufacturer

T-Bags

CDL Enterprises, Ltd.
4050 West Chandler Avenue
Santa Monica, California 92704
800-957-6288
www.t-bags.com

Soft luggage manufacturer

Touratech USA

701 34th Avenue
Seattle, Washington 98122
800-491-2926
www.touratech-usa.com

Supplier of a wide variety of motorcycle gear and camping equipment

Whitehorse Gear

107 East Conway Road
Center Conway, New Hampshire 03813
800-531-1133
www.whitehorsegear.com

Mail-order retailer of a wide variety of motorcycle gear, luggage, clothing, videos, and books

Willie & Max

4230 Clipper Drive
Manitowoc, Wisconsin 54220
800-558-7755
www.willieandmaxsaddlebags.com

Manufacturers of saddlebags and other luggage

Wolfman

2450 Central Avenue - Suite A
Boulder, Colorado 80301
800-535-8131; 303-541-9723
www.wolfmanluggage.com

Soft luggage

CAMPING AND CARGO TRAILERS

American Legend Motorcycle Trailers, Inc.
Mahomet, Illinois
888-463-1917
www.american-legend.com

B&F Specialties/Bunkhouse Trailers
Elk Grove Village, Illinois
847-350-9333
www.bf-specialties.com

Bushtec
Jacksboro, Tennessee
423-562-9900
www.bushtec.com

CyClemate
Edgerton, Minnesota
800-643-6237
www.cycle-mate.com

Hannigan Sidecars
Murray, Kentucky
270-753-4256
www.hannigansidecar.com

Kompact Kamp
Myerstown, Pennsylvania
717-933-8070
www.jdtrailers.com

M.W. Bourne
Marquez, Texas
903-529-3491
www.aerobourne.com

Motorvation Engineering
Sibley, Iowa
800-305-3664
www.motorvation.com

N-Line Trailers
Olive Branch, Mississippi
601-890-3952
www.n-line.com

Oldenkamp Inc.
Hull, Iowa
800-397-3819
www.oldinc.com

Scooter Schooner
Sharon, Oklahoma
800-628-9129
www.scooterschooner.com

Time Out Trailers, Inc.
Elkhart, Indiana
800-600-7671
www.timeouttrailers.org

Trailmaster
DesPlaines, Illinois
800-398-9090
www.trailmasterinc.com

Uni-Go, Ltd.
Christchurch, New Zealand
64-21-313-143
www.uni-go.com

Travel Bureaus

STATE OFFICES OF TOURISM

Washington, D.C.
www.washington.org

Alabama
800-252-2262
www.800alabama.com

Alaska
907-465-2012
www.travelalaska.com

Arizona
888-520-3434
www.arizonaguide.com

Arkansas
800-628-8725
www.arkansas.com

California
800-862-2543
www.visitcalifornia.com

Colorado
800-265-6723
www.colorado.com

Connecticut
800-282-6863
www.ctvisit.com

Delaware
800-441-8846
www.delaware.gov

Florida
888-735-2872
www.visitflorida.com

Georgia
800-847-4842
www.georgia.org

Hawaii
800-464-2924
www.gohawaii.com

Idaho
800-714-3246
www.visitidaho.org

Illinois
800-226-6632
www.enjoyillinois.com

Indiana
800-469-4612
www.in.gov/visitindiana

Iowa
800-345-4692
www.traveliowa.com

Kansas
800-252-6727
www.travelks.com

Kentucky
800-255-8747
www.kentuckytourism.com

Louisiana
800-334-8626
www.louisianatravel.com

Maine
888-624-6345
www.visitmaine.com

Maryland
800-634-7386
www.visitmaryland.org

Massachusetts
800-447-6277
www.massvacation.com

Michigan
888-784-7328
www.michigan.org

Minnesota
800-657-3700
www.exploreminnesota.com

Mississippi
800-927-6378
www.visitmississippi.org

Missouri
800-519-210
www.visitmo.com

Montana
800-847-4868
www.visitmt.com

Nebraska
800-228-4307
www.visitnebraska.gov

Nevada
800-237-0774
www.travelnevada.com

New Hampshire
800-386-4664
www.visitnh.gov

New Jersey
800-847-4865
www.state.nj.us/travel

New Mexico
800-733-6396
www.newmexico.org

New York
800-225-5697
www.iloveny.com

North Carolina
800-847-4862
www.visitnc.com

North Dakota
800-435-5663
www.ndtourism.com

Ohio
800-282-5393
www.ohiotourism.com

Oklahoma
800-652-6552
www.travelok.com

Oregon
800-547-7842
www.traveloregon.com

Pennsylvania
800-847-4872
www.visitpa.com

Rhode Island
800-556-2484
www.visitrhodeisland.com

South Carolina
800-810-5700
www.discoversouthcarolina.com

South Dakota
800-732-5682
www.travelsd.com

Tennessee
800-462-8366
www.tnvacation.com

Texas
800-888-8839
www.traveltexas.com

Utah
800-200-1600
www.utah.com

Vermont
800-837-6668
www.travel-vermont.com

Virginia
800-932-5827
www.virgina.org

Washington
800-544-1800
www.experiencewa.com

West Virginia
800-225-5982
www.callwva.com

Wisconsin
800-432-8747
www.travelwisconsin.com

Wyoming
800-225-5996
www.wyomingtourism.org

CANADIAN PROVINCIAL OFFICES OF TOURISM

Alberta
800-661-8888
www.travelalberta.com

British Columbia
800-435-5622
www.hellobc.com

Manitoba
800-665-0040
www.travelmanitoba.com

New Brunswick
800-561-0123
www.tourismnewbrunswick.ca

Newfoundland & Labrador
800-563-6353
www.newfoundlandlabrador.com

Nova Scotia
800-565-0000
www.novascotia.com

Ontario
800-668-2746; 416-314-0944
www.ontariotravel.net

Prince Edward Island
888-734-7529; 902-368-7795
www.tourismpei.com

Quebec
800-363-7777; 514-873-2015
www.bonjourquebec.com

Saskatchewan
877-237-2273; 306-787-2300
www.sasktourism.com

Yukon
www.travelyukon.com

CANADIAN GOVERNMENT OFFICES

Canadian Customs
www.cbsa-asfc.gc.ca

Canadian Firearms Centre
800-731-4000
www.rcmp.ca/cfp

Canadian Immigration
800-992-7037

Index